T0018006

MUSHROOM MAGICK

Ritual, Celebration, and Lore

SHAWN ENGEL

STERLING ETHOS
New York

STERLING ETHOS

New York

An Imprint of Sterling Publishing Co., Inc.

STERLING ETHOS and the distinctive Sterling Ethos logo are
registered trademarks of Sterling Publishing Co., Inc.

ISBN 978-1-4549-4448-5
978-1-4549-4449-2 (e-book)

For information about custom editions, special sales, and premium purchases,
please contact specialsales@unionsquareandco.com.

Printed in Malaysia

2 4 6 8 10 9 7 5 3

unionsquareandco.com

Cover design by Jo Obarowski Berger
Interior design by Gavin Motnyk
Interior illustrations by Lianne Pflug
Background textures from Shutterstock.com: captureandcompose, FOXARTBOX, Here, OLEGGANKO

For my love, a wildly fun-ghi who supports
even my most questionable morels.

CONTENTS

Introduction | 6

PART I
MUSHROOM GENERA AND SPECIES

PART II
MUSHROOM FOLKLORE ACROSS THE GLOBE

PART III
SPELLCASTING WITH FUNGI

Introduction

When we picture a mushroom, it's difficult to imagine an image as idyllic as the fantastical, red-capped, white polka-dotted toadstool of fairy tales. Yet that iconic, cute, fae-friendly fungus is just one of over 7,200 species of mushrooms in the world. Each one has its own energetic correspondences, ways of interacting with its environment, and place in tradition. Because mushrooms have held so much significance for so many cultures, folklore and fables surrounding these sometimes edible, sometimes toxic fungi are present all over the world. Whether these tales concern their interactions with elven folk, deities from nature, the dead, or other entities, mushrooms hold great sacred importance in many different places. And because of this, they are excellent to use in a variety of spells and rituals.

This guidebook aims to break down a small intersection of mushroom species: what they are, how they're used, their magickal properties, and what spells and intentions will be supported by them. Because there is such a breadth of mushrooms native to a plethora of lands, the distinction in size, shape, color, toxicity, and usage allow for many different energetic correspondences. Following a light overview of some of the most recognizable species and genera, you'll journey across numerous countries to see how different cultures use these vegetable-adjacent foods to see what aligns with your practice, while educating yourself on different applications and sacred rites.

Finally, this book will show you examples of different spells, rituals, and recipes to work into your own routine. No matter if you're a beginner practitioner, somewhat more intermediate, or a long-time, full-fledged witch, the final section of the book will be easy and practical to implement. And whether mushrooms become a cornerstone of your practice or simply a "once in a blue moon" addition, you'll be actively prepared to use household mushrooms by the end of this guide. Be warned, however, that if attempting to forage, you'd be wise to consult an expert in mycology, a scientist of fungi, as some of these beautiful pieces of nature are highly toxic, and some are even fatal.

PART 1

MUSHROOM GENERA AND SPECIES

When I was selecting the mushrooms for this guide, the task became overwhelming. There are an incredible number of genera and species of mushrooms. The mushrooms below are a just a few of the most common and have been selected to demonstrate a range of mystical properties. Feel free to use this collection as a mere starting point on your journey to understanding the vast and fantastic world of mushrooms.

The breakdown of mushroom identification is lengthy and somewhat hard to follow. To simplify: all mushrooms belong to the kingdom of Fungi, and are then broken down further, in succession, to a division, then class, then order, then family. This book, from the classification tree, focuses on both the genus and individual species. The genus is the umbrella to the individual species. I will be focusing on more specific types of mushrooms to give the best energetic correspondences possible.

AMANITA

What It Is

This is the most archetypal genus of mushroom, housing the species *Amanita muscaria*, or fly agaric, the iconic mushroom from Super Mario. However, there are several hundred species under this genus, typically characterized by the large white spores decorating the caps. This genus ranges from edible to poisonous to deadly, so foragers must be incredibly careful when searching for it in the wet summer and autumn months.

How It's Used

Since this is an entire genus, individual varietals are used in different ways depending upon features like color or edibility. For example, the

Caesar's mushroom, an edible *Amanita*, has been used in Italian cooking for over two thousand years, boasting a rich, nutty flavor. It pairs well with lemon juice, olive oil, and red wine vinegar as an addition to salads and is also delicious grilled and sautéed. This genus also houses the more popular psychoactive species, although these are not recommended for consumption. It would be wise for anyone attempting to consume these mushrooms to rule out whether or not they are fatal and to consult with an expert before even touching them.

Magickal Properties

Because of their alignment with the fae, elven folk, and other mystical forest dwellers, mushrooms of this genus are often used to strengthen magick. They have earthly and grounding properties, and depending on the particular species, can be used in edible applications for divination. More potent and poisonous species may be of use for baneful magick and hexing. All in all, this entire genus is an amplifier for any spell the practitioner chooses but is most potent in wards and protection.

How to Use in Spells

As with all mushrooms, but particularly this genus, toxicity must be taken into account before delving into spellwork. Edible species are appropriate for kitchen witchery, in which case the practitioner may imbue the mushroom's intention into the recipe. These mushrooms are most aligned with magick and divination and may be consumed before performing a reading. The poisonous varietals, however, are best used with caution in spell jars specifically for hexing. One may put a photo of their subject in a jar with a nail through the mushroom and the picture to perform a baneful spell. Proceed with caution, ethics, and morals, however, as this is a very potent hexing tool.

FLY AGARIC (*Amanita muscaria*)
What It Is

One of the most archetypal species of mushrooms, it is often depicted as a toadstool fungus with large, white gills, white spots, and a red cap. This species is iconic; no doubt you've seen a watercolor painting of a fairy sitting atop one, or merely noticed one when you played Super Mario as a kid. Said to be a cosmopolitan species, meaning that it spans most climates (in both the Southern and Northern hemispheres), it also engages in symbiosis (a close relationship between unassociated biological organisms—think Nemo and anemones from *Finding Nemo*) with pine and birch plantations.

How It's Used

While *Amanita muscaria* is a psychoactive, it is highly toxic and poisonous. One of the reasons for this is that it houses the biologically active agent muscimol and ibotenic acid, which is an amino acid. This was discovered in the mid-twentieth century by researchers in England, Japan, and Switzerland. In Siberia, however, aboriginal shamans would use it to achieve a trance state (with much training under their belt) and have their followers consume their (i.e., the shamans') urine to achieve trance by proxy. Aside from other cultural importance relating to its psychoactive properties—which we will revisit in the following section—it also has a few culinary uses. Spanning Europe, North America, and parts of Japan, the mushroom is detoxified by chefs by parboiling it in water, as the toxins of this genus are water soluble. From there, *Amanita muscaria* is then either soaked in vinegar to make a steak sauce, or pickled and salted as is done in the Nagano Prefecture region of Japan.

Magickal Properties

The agaric mushroom is widely known as symbolic of an enchanted forest, attracting fairies and gnomes. Because of its psychoactive properties, we can see how indigenous cultures came to this conclusion! This particular genus is also associated with the element of air and the planet Mercury, and, coupled with its intoxicating properties, is said to aid in dream work, psychic work, and intention setting. However, I do not suggest ingesting to receive this energetic boost. In addition, use of this particular mushroom is excellent in fertility spells, but again, not by means of consumption.

How to Use in Spells

When working with this mushroom, you may want to add it to spell jars to promote pregnancy or even a creative birth such as a new project or business. In addition, placing one under your pillow can aid in dreamwork. Drying this mushroom may also help with divination when it is placed on your altar or near your tarot deck, runes, or oracle cards. If you wish to work with the fae, this is also a great offering.

GREEN AMANITA (*Amanita phalloides*)
What It Is

A toxic mushroom, green amanita is also known by the cryptic name of the death cap. Found mostly across Europe, this highly poisonous mushroom forms with broad-leaved trees such as oak or chestnut and pine during the summer months. Although this organism resembles edible mushrooms, such as Caesar's and straw mushrooms, it can be distinguished by its generally (though not always) green cap, white stripe, and gills. So, when mushroom foraging, it is wise to consult an expert before consumption, as the results could be deadly.

How It's Used

There are no known uses of *Amanita phalloides* because of its extreme toxicity. Six to twenty-four hours after ingestion it attacks the liver, requiring medical attention and commonly hospitalization. Consumption of this mushroom often results in death. Unfortunately, because of its non-threatening appearance, sweet aroma, and (some report) delicious taste, it is very important to proceed with caution when foraging, even when touching with one's bare hands.

Magickal Properties

Because of its benign appearance and inviting smell, this particular mushroom houses many metaphysical properties fit for baneful magick. It has energetic cloaking capabilities, as well as protective qualities. While this organism must never be consumed, or even sought out, if one were to come across this varietal, it could assist in a variety of hexes.

How to Use in Spells

Again, stressing that this mushroom shouldn't be eaten under any circumstances, one can (if procured safely) use this as a tool for support in protection. Stuffed in a spell jar to enhance a return-to-sender spell, it can be incredibly potent. Alternately, if placed in a jar situated near entryways of the home, it can help to keep out harmful energy. It is very wise, however, to only use this mushroom in sealed-jar spells, for if it were to be consumed by a child or an animal, the results could be devastating. Please proceed with caution.

BUTTON (*Agaricus bisporus*)
What It Is

This is a small, white bulbous-looking button, hence its name. Grown year round, this fungus is native to the grasslands of Europe and North America. Very commonly used in food, this mushroom is obviously edible; however, when foraging, one should be cautious of its poisonous look-alike, known as the "destroying angel," distinguishable by the pure white gills on the cap, as opposed to the light brown gills of the button mushroom. Closely related to the cremini and portobello, the button mushroom is the youngest of this genus.

How It's Used

As the most common mushroom used in cuisine, this fungus is often referred to as a table mushroom. A chef may use it baked, grilled, raw, roasted, or otherwise, as it is extremely versatile. You may have seen it on your favorite New York slice of pizza, or on a skewer at a neighbor's barbecue. Culturally, these mushrooms have a rich background. In Egypt, they were revered for consumption and thought to give metaphysical powers or even eternal life. They were also used in traditional Chinese medicine to balance the body's energy and promote overall health.

Magickal Properties

Still cultivated underground in West France to this day, button mushrooms were once found in the catacombs of Paris, leading the French to believe they were associated with the dead. Because mushrooms spring from the ground as a species, this is a very common belief. As stated above, however, this mushroom, much like the ouroboros, signified immortality to ancient Egyptians. Because of its small, young, pure white appearance growing as a fungus, it is easy to see the symbolism of the life-death cycle in this organism.

How to Use in Spells

This may be the most readily available mushroom when it comes to performing kitchen witchery. Add this into any recipe for an energy reset, or even for the blessing of vitality, with a nod to the Egyptians. Because this particular genus is possibly the most obvious symbol of life and death, this would be another great offering for spirit work and mediumship. As a grief ritual, one may place this on an altar and pray for the safe passage of a soul who has moved on.

CREMINI (*Agaricus bisporous*)
What It Is

The cremini is an *Agaricus bisporous* like the white button mushroom or the portobello, but slightly more mature than the former and less mature than the latter. Because of the cremini's maturation, it has a browner color, firmer texture, and better flavor than the white button. It also holds up much better in liquid than its younger counterpart. Cremini mushrooms have small, brown gills;

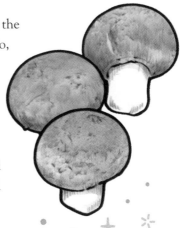

however, the gills are mostly hidden underneath the cap, as they have not fully opened when harvested at the cremini stage. *Agaricus bisporous* account for about ninety percent of all of the mushrooms cultivated in the United States, and they are a favorite in the kitchen.

How It's Used
Cremini mushrooms are incredibly versatile because of their firm texture. Used both raw and cooked, this varietal can be used in anything from salads to stews and can also be stuffed or baked. These mushrooms can also be kept fresh for about a week when properly stored, for example in a paper bag with a moist towel when refrigerated to maintain its integrity without overmoisturizing.

Magickal Properties
Grown since ancient times, this mushroom is aligned with many magickal properties across the globe. As with the button mushroom, the Egyptians believed these mushrooms gave special powers to those who consumed them, including immortality. The Romans deemed this mushroom as a "food of the gods," while the French associated this varietal with the dead, as they grew in the catacombs of Paris. Additionally, the Chinese and Koreans used cremini mushrooms to increase milk production for breast feeding, leading us to associate *Agaricus bisporus* with the triple goddess: the white button is the maiden, cremini is the mother, and portobello is the crone.

How to Use in Spells

Because of its association with the mother archetype, this is a great mushroom for fertility spells. Cremini is aligned with the breasts, so it can be used for both glamour spells and spells related to motherhood. One may use this for kitchen witchery with the intention of cooking this energy into a recipe, or consuming on its own with a sigil carved into the cap. Additionally, as the ancient beliefs suggest, this mushroom can also be used for vitality spells and amplification of energy. The best way to use cremini mushrooms for these intentions is by consumption.

PORTOBELLO (*Agaricus bisporous*)
What It Is

The final maturation of *Agaricus bisporous* (the other two being the button and cremini mushrooms), this mushroom is large in size, with the cap measuring an average fifteen centimeters (about six inches) in diameter. The rounded flat cap and thick stem is firm and spongy, ranging in hue from dark brown to tan. There are dark brown, fleshy gills underneath the caps, which also house a small ring from the spongy white veil. Native around the Northern Hemisphere, these mushrooms grow individually in grass near manure piles and on leaf litter near conifers such as Monterey cypress trees.

How It's Used

Used mainly in the kitchen, this mushroom is great for sautéing, grilling, and broiling. Because of the larger, matured caps, they can be used as a meat substitute in burgers and hollowed out as pizza crust or an edible bowl. Native to Italy, this mushroom is used in many popular Italian dishes. The rich, meatlike texture and savory, earthy notes make portobellos a favorite ingredient of home and professional chefs alike.

Magickal Properties

As stated in the entries for button and cremini mushrooms, this is the final maturation of the genus—meaning, this particular organism is aligned with the Crone archetype. While excellent for grounding and connecting with the sacral chakra, this mushroom is also aligned with wisdom, age, maturity, and even death. Because the Crone archetype is symbolized by a waning moon, this mushroom has releasing qualities, great for transformation and hexing.

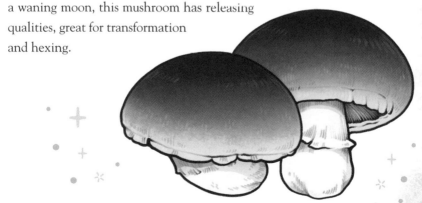

How to Use in Spells

If desiring to use this mushroom in kitchen witchcraft, you might consume it during a waning moon phase to initiate a cord-cutting spell, severing old attachments and opening you up to new relationships and experiences. This is also a great mushroom to devour before engaging in divination. One may also eat this mushroom with the intention of increasing wisdom before embarking on a new journey, or as an aid in a spell jar for the same purpose. Finally, if the practitioner works with the triple goddess archetypes, such as Hekate, Kali, or the Fates, one may use this as an altar offering. For hygienic purposes, watch that the mushroom does not turn; however, if it does, it will not affect the spell or offering, as transformation is a key energetic property.

LACTARIUS

What It Is

Lactarius, a genus of mushrooms that contains the indigo milk cap (page 24), is characterized by the latex, or "milk," that the fruiting bodies produce. There are more than five hundred known species all over the Northern Hemisphere that contain this distinguished ooze. While most of the specimens in this group secrete a white or cream color latex, there are other specimens known to have more brightly colored milk, such

as the indigo milk cap mushroom and the red pine. The fruit bodies range from small to very large and are fleshy with gills under the often-depressed cap. Most of the species in this genus are edible; however, some can be quite toxic, although not deadly poisonous.

How It's Used

Because of the edibility of the majority of its species, this mushroom genus is generally used for flavorings and sold at outdoor markets around the world. While not appropriate for drying, because of the milk produced, edible milk mushrooms can be used for marinades and sauces. There are some small, fragrant species, affectionately named "candy caps," that are used for this purpose. The blue milk, being a more brightly colored species, is often used to add color to a dish.

Magickal Properties

Color magick plays a role in this mushroom's metaphysical properties. The *Lactarius indigo* is excellent for communication. The orange species, known as *L. deliciosus*, is aligned with creativity and joy. Some species grow pinkish spores, and those would be complementary to self-love and affection. The practitioner has a range of possibilities with this genus, depending on how and where it is sourced.

How to Use in Spells

The most special quality of the "milk" genus is the latex produced by all of its species, so in order to effectively harness the energy, the latex should be front and center in your spells. Sure, you can eat these mushrooms, put them in a jar, or use them for kitchen witchcraft, but the magick is in the milk for this category of fungi, so using the latex will amplify any spell. Anointing your candles, jars, or other spellwork with the milk will help alchemize the intended energy. Align your spells with the color of the milk chosen, like white for purity, blue for communication, orange for creation, and so on.

INDIGO MILK CAP (*Lactarius indigo*)

What It Is

Also called the blue milk mushroom, the indigo milk cap is identifiable by its gorgeous blue cap and gills. While the colors will range from a pale gray blue in matured specimens to a deep blue or violet in fresher ones, the defining hue is what gives it its name. This particular mushroom is edible; however, there are varying opinions on whether or not the taste is desirable. Found on the ground of deciduous and coniferous forests, this widely distributed species can be found across North America, East Asia, and Central America.

How It's Used

As stated above, although the blue milk mushroom is edible, its taste is controversial. Some state that it is a superior mushroom, while others believe it is far from it. Regardless, its slightly bitter and peppery taste is best when the firm flesh is sliced. When the mushroom is cooked, the blue dissipates and becomes a milky gray. The latex, or "milk," that the fruiting body produces is also blue, but when exposed to air it eventually turns a shade of green, which is used to add some color to marinades. While this mushroom doesn't lend itself to drying because of its granular flesh, it is popular in Mexican, Guatemalan, and Chinese markets, where it is sold fresh.

Magickal Properties

Because of its incredible blue color, the indigo milk cap holds excellent communicative properties. Aligning with the mind, wit, connection, and conversation, this mushroom is excellent for opening the throat chakra. Similarly, because of the deeper and richer hue of the fresher organisms, they can promote psychic connection.

How to Use in Spells

One can perform a variety of spells with this species. For example, a practitioner may choose to eat this mushroom before having a tough conversation while focusing on the throat chakra, providing courage and the freedom of vulnerability. One may also use the milk of this mushroom to anoint a candle or other altar offering to open communication. In addition, before practicing divination, one may want to consume the younger specimen to open their third eye to psychic abilities.

BEECH (*Hypsizygus tesselatus*)

What It Is

This edible mushroom is found growing on beech trees; hence, the name. Although native to East Asia, this genus is also cultivated in Europe, North America, and Australia. They naturally grow on wood, engaging in symbiosis, and have a small, thin, gilled appearance with a white or brown cap. Most popularly used in cooking, beech mushrooms have two

different variations, designated by their color, being either brown beech mushrooms and brown clamshell mushrooms, or white beech mushrooms and white clamshell mushrooms.

How It's Used

Falling under the umbrella of Japanese shimeji mushrooms, this genus is known as one of most prized fungi by gourmets. Firm and bitter when uncooked but delicious after being sautéed or boiled, beech mushrooms are often used in soups, stews, and sauces to add a crunchy texture with a mildly sweet and nutty flavor. Most popularly used in ramen, stir-fry, and rice, this mushroom is extremely versatile. This particular genus is also said to have anticancer properties because of beta-glucan, which reduces inflammation in the body.

Magickal Properties

Because of the beech mushrooms' biological makeup, it has extremely potent metaphysical properties. Because they contain selenium, a powerful antioxidant, beech mushrooms are known to be excellent for cleansing. As an anti-inflammatory nutritional aid, this mushroom also connects with the heart and sacral energy centers. Finally, and most magickally of all, this genus contains copper, which is an excellent energy conduit known to heal in the physical plane and help to connect with the spiritual realm.

How to Use in Spells

Beech mushrooms are great for kitchen witchery! Using them intentionally in recipes can help you open up your heart chakra and increase passion. Similarly, you can use them in any recipe to add a cleansing element to your spell. You can also place them on your altar to connect with your ancestors. To give them extra oomph, place them on top of or with copper jewelry, coins, or bowls.

BLACK TRUMPET (*Craterellus cornucopioides*)

Another edible mushroom, it is also known as the horn of plenty, black chanterelle, or trumpet of the dead. Peeling out like a lily flower, which is also associated with the dead, this mushroom is unique in that it has no gills, teeth, or pores. Black and gray in appearance, this genus can grow between four and six inches (ten to fifteen centimeters), and because it tends to grow in moss and moist spots in the woods (namely in Europe, North America, Korea, and Japan) it is said to symbolize the dead and buried playing a horn from beneath the soil.

How It's Used

Also used in cooking, this genus is a favorite of chefs because of its distinct flavor. It has an extremely delicate, smoky profile, making it great to pair with a multitude of foods. Known also as the "poor man's truffle," one can use this to add extra flavor to any recipe without overpowering it. Perfect with any recipe that calls for white wine, such as any fish or garlic preparation, you're sure to enjoy this absolute delicacy.

Magickal Properties

Because of the color and lore surrounding this mushroom, it has incredible mystical properties. Referring to its Latin name, this mushroom is associated with the cornucopia, which was known to magickally fill itself with whatever meat or drink its owner requested. Belonging to Amalthea's goat (or herself in goat form), the cornucopia has become a symbol of abundance, and likewise, so has this mushroom. Interestingly, aside from its ability to aid in manifesting dreams, it is also an offering for protection received from the dead. Because of its color and association with spirits, it is a very mystical fungus.

How to Use in Spells

It would be wise for the practitioner to use this beauty in kitchen witchery, because it is delicious! Adding to any recipe will increase abundance. However, if you want to approach the more mysterious side of this mushroom, you could use it in a recipe by setting its intention for divination. Similarly, practitioners can place this mushroom on an ancestral altar to bridge a connection between themselves and ancestors or people who have passed. Crumbling and keeping this genus in a vessel or near a deck of tarot cards can also increase psychic protection.

BLACK SADDLE MUSHROOM (*Helvella lacunosa*)
What It Is
Also called the fluted black elfin saddle, this is an irregularly shaped black-and-gray mushroom with a fluted stem and a fuzzy underside. Its cap is wrinkled in an almost deflated fashion. The full fungi grow anywhere from half an inch to four inches (one and one-half to ten centimeters). There is debate as to whether this genus is edible, as some cultures regard it highly for cooking, though only the cap is edible, never the stem; please consult an expert. However, some toxicity is found in its biological makeup. Most common in North America, it is also found in Europe, Japan, and China under pine, oak, and Douglas fir.

How It's Used
Although this genus is most commonly used in cooking, it should be noted that great care should be used, and experts need to be consulted

prior to preparation. It is necessary to parboil the fungus for three to five minutes to release any toxicity, discarding the water when finished. One may also dry or pickle this mushroom, although when pickling, it is necessary to first parboil the mushroom as well. When drying, the toxicity will be released into the air. It is also interesting to note that a dark pigment may be released during cooking, depending on the mushroom.

Magickal Properties

As an oddly shaped mushroom with toxic attributes and a dark to black shade, this fungus has excellent protective energy. Aligned with the Druids, these mushrooms are also associated with transformation and magick. Because it is referred to as the elfin saddle, and elves are said to be mystical and nature-based spirits possessed with immortality (much like fairies), this mushroom is also associated with vitality.

How to Use in Spells

If there was ever a mushroom fit for a hex, this would be your go-to. Throw this fungus in a spell jar to add some kick to your baneful magick. Additionally, because of its pigment, it is perfect for divination and connecting to the spirit realm. Similarly, when working with darker deities and crone goddesses such as Baba Yaga, Hekate, Kali, or Lilith, one can place this on a worship altar or in an offering bowl. And finally, if the practitioner is properly trained, she may also use this in a cooking recipe with the intention of youth and strength. Add it into a rice dish for vitality, but be sure to parboil with caution!

CHANTERELLE
What It Is
The common name of several species of edible mushrooms, the family of chanterelle are classified by their meaty, funnel shape and smooth cap with forked folds. Although they vary in color from orange to yellow to white, most look like flowers, even marigolds, springing from the ground. The name originates from the Greek *kantharos*, meaning "vase," referring to their shape. Another wild fungus that engages in symbiosis, while chanterelles are found across the globe, they are difficult to commercially cultivate, as there is a lack of flavor when one tries to re-create the relationship with the host plant. You will find chanterelles near maple, poplar, birch, and oak.

How It's Used

This mushroom has a very sweet, apricot-like aroma and a peppery taste, making it a beautiful addition to many dishes. Because chanterelles are generally meatier and richer than cultivated mushrooms, they work best with sautéing, boiling, frying, or as an addition to rich sauces. Growing in the wild since ancient times, they have been sought after as a delicacy across Europe, from Greece to Russia to Germany, where they are referred to as *Pfifferlinge*.

Magickal Properties

Because this fungus engages in symbiosis, it is excellent in spells to strengthen relationships. Being aligned with the water element, this organism is also great for connecting with intuition, emotion, and psychic abilities. Its golden hue aligns it with the sun and renders it symbolic of solar energy, which means it is very effective for spells related to the summer solstice. Finally, used for medicinal purposes, this mushroom is anti-inflammatory, antimicrobial, and an antioxidant.

How to Use in Spells

This mushroom is great for love spells, if one is included for this purpose. Whether the practitioner uses it intentionally when cooking for their love, or places it in a spell jar, the energy is excellent for bonding. One could also use this in a recipe to strengthen intuition, or place it on one's altar to create a divinatory environment. Similarly, one could use it on an altar to call in the energy from the sun or increase creativity. And if one would like to call in its healing properties, the practitioner can speak this intention into a tea made from this mushroom and drink it.

ENOKI (*Flammulina velutipes*)
What It Is

Enoki is an edible mushroom popular in Japanese cuisine. It is also known as the velvet shank. It grows naturally on the stumps of trees such as Chinese hackberry, ash, mulberry, and persimmon. It is a winter fungus because it grows during the months of September through March. This particular varietal ranges in color and texture, depending on whether it was harvested wild or cultivated, as the lack of light in cultivation results in a white color, whereas wild enoki presents in shades of gold, orange, and brown. Known for its long stem, small cap, and growth in clusters, this mushroom must not be mistaken with the similar-looking but poisonous *Galerina marginata* (the funeral bell or deadly skullcap mushroom). Care is advised and an expert must be consulted if wild foraging is undertaken.

How It's Used

The enoki mushroom is known for its al dente texture; firm, crunchy bite; and mild, fruity flavor. While these mushrooms can be eaten both raw and cooked, it is important to trim and discard the ends, wash the mushrooms, and throw out any slimy pieces to retain the integrity of the crunch. Although most commonly used in hot pot recipes to add texture, there are a variety of recipes appropriate for the enoki. In addition to cooking, these mushrooms have been popularly used in Chinese, Japanese, and Korean medicinal practices. The Japanese are known to make enoki ice, where the fungus is boiled and poured into ice cube trays to make teas, soups, and curries.

Magickal Properties

Because it is rich in vitamins and minerals, this mushroom is used in medicine and is known to have healing properties. When working with the cultivated varietal, one that is white and long stemmed, the energies involved include purification and cleansing.

How to Use in Spells

As a popular edible species, this mushroom is great for kitchen witchery, again by infusing intention as you cook. One may make a tea for cleansing and healing, or use the mushroom in a soup when sick. Pairing this mushroom with similarly potent ingredients, such as garlic and lemon, will help to amplify the healing benefits in whichever recipe you desire. Because this mushroom is also grown during colder months, this is great as an offering for the winter solstice, or for rebirth and transformation.

HEDGEHOG (*Hydnum repandum*)
What It Is
This is a large-capped edible mushroom also known as the sweet tooth or wood hedgehog. Characterized by its spore-bearing spines that hang from the underside of the irregularly shaped cap, this fungus ranges in color from yellow to orange to light brown. Found all over Europe near either cone-bearing seed plants or woodland that experiences seasonal shedding by streams or rivers, this edible fungus has a slightly spicy and bitter taste. Fortunately for foragers, this mushroom has no known poisonous doppelgangers.

How It's Used
Generally used in culinary applications, this mushroom is great sautéed on its own, or added to soups, stews, and sauces. It is also a great substitute for chanterelle mushrooms because of its similar taste and texture. They can also be used for canning and pickling. Hedgehog mushrooms pair well with bay leaves, fresh herbs, and garlic. They also have a medicinal

quality. In addition, the more brightly colored specimens of this particular fungus can be used to dye wool. And finally, this is a great training mushroom for novice foragers since there is no known toxic lookalike.

Magickal Properties

Associated with sheep by the French, who dubbed them *pied-de-mouton*, or "foot of the sheep," not only does this fungus have grounding properties, but it also has energies of peace, purity, community, and dedication. This mushroom, because of where it's grown, is also aligned with the element of water. Containing anti-inflammatory and antibacterial properties, this varietal is also incredibly healing.

How to Use in Spells

Sufficient to use in many different spells, as always, its edibility makes it great for kitchen witchcraft. By setting an intention when cooking, emphasizing any of the aforementioned qualities, you can infuse your meals with magick. Because of this mushroom's use as dye in certain cultures, it is also great to use for glamour magick. By intentionally picking an intentional color, one can infuse a garment with energetic properties. Finally, to make an incredibly potent healing tea or broth, one can infuse the mushroom in water with garlic and a bay leaf to call in wellness.

HEN OF THE WOODS (*Grifola frondosa*)

What It Is

Also called maitake, this mushroom is native to China, Europe, and North America. It is known as a polypore mushroom, which describes a large fruiting body with gills and one to three pores on its underside—it's a unique-looking mushroom. It is also an important culinary ingredient in China and Japan. However, there are a few poisonous look-alikes that foragers should beware of; please consult an expert before foraging. Sprouting from a potato-sized sclerotium (the resting spore that generates a fungus), this organism can grow up to sixty inches (152 centimeters) in a shape reminiscent of a coral reef.

How It's Used

These edible delicacies have a rich flavor and texture. They are meaty and slightly firm, with smoky, earthy flavors and notes of clove, ginger, and cinnamon. Because maitakes have an incredibly short shelf life, chefs often prefer working with dried ones, as they will hold flavor for much longer. With their unique biological makeup and antibacterial properties, these mushrooms have been used medicinally as well, whether in capsule form, as a tonic, or in teas.

Magickal Properties

Because of its medicinal properties, this mushroom has a healing energy.

However, because of the notes in its flavor palette, and of its history in medieval Japan as currency (it was once exchanged for silver), this mushroom also houses qualities related to abundance. When a large grouping was found, foragers would dance with joy, leading to the Japanese name *maitake*, which translates to "dancing mushroom." Hen of the woods is also aligned with egg-laying poultry, which symbolizes abundance. Additionally, since it has yet another alternate animal-related name, the ram's head, it also carries this animal's symbolism and is accordingly aligned with creativity and persistence.

How to Use in Spells

As with other edible mushrooms, this mushroom is great for kitchen witchcraft. When infusing one's intention into a recipe, one can call in the energies listed above. However, I would highly suggest using this mushroom to attract abundance. If desired, one can boil a pot (or cauldron) of these mushrooms with other abundant herbs, like cinnamon, cloves, and anise, and let the steam permeate your hearth. This can also stimulate creativity when needed.

HONEY AGARIC
(*Armillaria tabescens*)
What It Is

Armillaria is a genus of fungi that describes some of the largest living organisms in the world, categorizing mushrooms that live on trees and woody shrubs that can cover more than 3.4 square miles (5.5 square kilometers). Rather than engaging in symbiosis with the organisms it grows on, this fungus is actually parasitic, causing "white rot" root disease. However, unlike parasites that must keep their host alive in order to feed, this particular organism can feed on dead plant material, making it able to survive regardless of host health.

How It's Used

This mushroom is regarded as a delicacy in many European countries, including Ukraine, Russia, Poland, and Germany. However, it must be noted that this wild varietal is slightly poisonous in its raw form, so it would behoove the chef to cook this mushroom thoroughly. Furthermore, even when the mushroom is cooked, it is possible to suffer nausea and indigestion when it is consumed with alcohol, which is why it is advised not to drink alcohol for twelve hours before and twenty-four hours after eating the honey agaric. That being said, this highly regarded treat has a delicious earthy and nutty flavor.

Magickal Properties

Because of its parasitic nature, this mushroom has a few interesting vampiric qualities. Whereas many mushrooms are aligned with healing, this varietal happens to be energy draining, making it appropriate for baneful magick. This mushroom soaks up energy like a sponge, so it's wise to proceed with caution when using it for spell casting.

How to Use in Spells

This fungus is perfect for performing a binding spell. While not necessarily encouraged or advised, it is up to the practitioner's discretion of whether or not to perform this type of magick. When placed in a jar next to a photo of the subject, the parasitic energy of this organism will do the work needed to drain power from your target. In addition, if cooking this mushroom appropriately and without the consumption of alcohol, one can use it in kitchen witchery by serving it to one's subject. Again, caution is urged and binding spells are not advised, but this is the preferred genus for that particular magick.

KING TRUMPET (*Pleurotus eryngii*)

What It Is

Also called the French horn mushroom, this is an edible oyster mushroom found in the Mediterranean regions of Europe, the Middle

East, North Africa, and many parts of Asia. Distinguished by its flat cap and thick round stem, king trumpets grow from medium to large in size, about eight inches (twenty centimeters) in length, and have short, off-white gills. They are naturally weak and parasitic, feeding off the roots of herbaceous plants in hot desert or humid climates.

How It's Used

While rare to find in the wild, these mushrooms are quite popular in Chinese and Japanese cuisine. The king trumpet is grown in a culture of agricultural waste, like sawdust and straw, supplemented by cottonseed meal and grain by-products. Because they have a dense, chewy texture and seafoodlike flavor, they are best used in stir-fries and tempura. In addition, this chewy and steaklike mushroom is known to be a meat substitute, where a "scallop" is created and cooked in butter and wine.

Magickal Properties

Because it is rarely grown in the wild and also used as a meat alternative, this particular organism has many glamour and cloaking properties. Being engineered, for lack of a better term, in cultivation makes this mushroom a conduit for alchemy. When found wild, because of its slightly parasitic nature and affinity for hot climates, this mushroom has binding and vampiric qualities as well.

How to Use in Spells

Because of its wide range of properties, this mushroom has many different applications for its practitioner. Because it is edible, one may consume this organism for beauty and glamour spells. King trumpet mushrooms can also be used as an accelerator in abundance spells, being placed on an altar, in a jar, or in a meal for kitchen witchcraft. If found wild, this mushroom can be used in a spell jar for binding, with hot sauce or other heat-giving ingredients added to give some kick to one's baneful magick.

MOREL (*Morchella esculenta*)
What It Is

Morchella, another genus of mushrooms, are characterized by their striking honeycomb appearance, created by a system of their caps intricately weaved in a cluster. There is much controversy about the species underlying this genus, with some mycologists stating there are as few as three species, while others claim there are up to thirty. Because of their affinity to temperate climates, these mushrooms are found wild in North America, Turkey, China, the Himalayas, India, Pakistan, and Kashmir, and are highly sought after as a delicacy in French cuisine.

How It's Used

Extreme care must be taken when foraging for these mushrooms, as eating false morels can result in severe reactions such as fever, convulsions, and even coma and death. Consult an expert before using morels. Because morels have a very short season in spring, their rarity makes them not only a prized find for chefs, but also the subject of a popular springtime activity for foragers. Hundreds gather for a National Morel Mushroom Festival in Boyne City, Michigan, which has been going on for a century. Because of the morel's deep, earthy flavor, it is often featured as a luxurious component of dishes in fine dining restaurants. However, these mushrooms should not be consumed raw, as they are naturally toxic, but they can be carefully sautéed or fried to remove the poison.

Magickal Properties

Because of its scarcity, its appearance, and its association with the season of spring, this mushroom is very aligned with the Greek goddess Persephone. It is said in folklore that Persephone was kidnapped by Hades, who took her to the underworld to marry. As Hades wished for utter devotion, he fed her a pomegranate, which tied her to his realm permanently. Persephone's mother, Demeter, forbade the earth from bearing fruit until she returned from the underworld, plunging the world into famine, so eventually Hades agreed to a compromise in which Persephone would spend half the year back in the world of the living, returning to her mother each spring. The symbolism of the pomegranate (which, when eaten, has a honeycomb appearance) and spring make this mushroom perfect for goddess work.

How to Use in Spells

If one works with Persephone, this would be a great offering for her altar. Because she is a harbinger of spring, this mushroom is also an excellent offering on the pagan festival Ostara, or the spring equinox. Persephone is a maiden, fair and pure, but she is also the Queen of the Underworld, which is why this mushroom is great for spirit work. If consuming this delicacy, set an intention to commune with the dead, and your energy will be amplified.

OYSTER (*Pleurotus ostreatus*)

What It Is

A popular edible mushroom characterized by its fanlike cap and little to no stem, the oyster's flesh is white, meaty, and firm. Its white gills extend from the cap. This mushroom ranges in color from dark gray, brown, tan, pink, and yellow. It is available year round and has a slightly fennel-like aroma, with a mild, nutty, and seafoodlike flavor. Stacking in a shelflike formation on dying wood, particularly beech and aspen, this mushroom gets its name from its uncanny similarities to freshly shucked oysters.

How It's Used

Originally cultivated in Germany during World War I as a subsistence food, it's now commercially grown around the world. This organism is great for cooking, particularly frying, and is used frequently in Asian cuisine, particularly in Japan, China, and Korea. However, that is not the most interesting thing about this category of fungi. This particular mushroom is carnivorous, feeding on bacteria and nematodes, and is used to organically clean decaying environments. When an oyster mushroom aids dying wood in decomposition, this helps clean the ecosystem.

Magickal Properties

This mushroom's magickal properties heavily depend on its color. Gray, brown, and tan mushrooms will align with grounding; the pink shades will allow for self-love and affection; and the yellow varietals will aid in intelligence and confidence. However, because of its carnivorous spirit, it is also an excellent tool for regeneration and transformation. Further, its ability to clean its environment naturally results in a purifying energy.

How to Use in Spells

Because this mushroom is edible, kitchen witchcraft is preferable for this organism. Consume the darker colors before mediation for grounding, the pinker shades for glamour, romance, and self-love, and the yellower shades for mental clarity. One may also place this mushroom as an offering on an altar to cleanse the practitioner's space, while being conscious of its short shelf life. Finally, if the practitioner is at a crossroads, consumption of these mushrooms will help accelerate one's journey to the next phase.

PORCINI (*Boletus edulis*)

What It Is

Also known as the penny bun, this mushroom is a favorite in European countries, especially Italy. Known affectionately by the French as *cèpes* and by the Germans as *Steinpilz*, these edible fungi are known for the spores that fill the underside of the cap like cotton, rather than possessing gills. They are firm when fresh and absorb a great deal of moisture so, when cleaning, minimal water should be used. Slightly sticky to the touch, these mushrooms are widely distributed in the Northern Hemisphere, and while not indigenous to the Southern Hemisphere, they have been introduced to southern Africa, Australia, New Zealand, and Brazil.

How It's Used

Mainly used for cooking, this versatile fungus is great in many dishes. Because they are slippery, they are most commonly sautéed, preserved, or dried. Drying a brown-cap can be done in a number of ways, including by blanching before simply hanging in the kitchen.

Magickal Properties

This particular genus is associated with abundance, strength, and prosperity because of its growth in deciduous forests. The most prevalent trees in folk magick are oak and maple trees, which are instrumental in the different sabats of the pagan Wheel of the Year, namely the winter and summer solstices. Because this is a very popular mushroom in Italy, it is associated with Italian folk magick.

How to Use in Spells

A popular mushroom in the kitchen, a practitioner can use this to add in abundant energy to a dish. However, one can also consume store-bought porcinis raw with the intention of manifesting. Because a method of treatment is to dry this mushroom by hanging it, one can also make a garland of these mushrooms and set an intention for each piece when preparing to hang. To bring strength and prosperity into the home via folk magick, hang this garland over the threshold of the kitchen.

RUSSULA

What It Is

The genus *Russula* has many brightly capped species under it. *Russula emetica*, also known as the sickener, is one of the most prominent of the approximately 750 species under this genus. While they are related to the *Lactarius* genus, they do not emit the milk that *Lactarius* is known for, and instead are

characterized by amyloid ornamented spores that, untouched, range from white to dark yellow, and, when anointed with iodine, will change to a stark black or blue. This genus is widespread across the Northern Hemisphere, including Britain, Ireland, mainland Europe, and also northern Africa.

How It's Used

Since this genus accounts for five percent of the world's known fungi, there are a variety of uses for it, depending on the species in question. For example, the *Russula emetica*, or the vomiting russula, is not edible and can make one very sick if ingested, although it is not known to be proven fatal. When one is foraging, these mushrooms are quite distinguishable by their brightly colored caps and size, but because of the breadth of species under this genus, it is wise to proceed with caution.

Magickal Properties

Again, since there are a wealth of mushrooms that constitute the genus *Russula*, there are very many uses, depending on the properties of the species. The two categories one would look for if seeking magickal properties are edibility and color. For example, the sickener, while not edible, is red in color, so one can surmise that its energetic properties are packed with intense repelling properties. On the other hand, *Russula chloroide*, or the blue-band brittle-gilled mushroom, an edible species, is great for strengthening communication and opening the throat chakra.

How to Use in Spells

By proceeding with caution and identifying the edibility of the species one is working with, the practitioner may either use the mushroom in a spell jar or in kitchen witchcraft. The edibility and color will allow the practitioner to decide how and when to work with the species, noting that, regardless of either category, these mushrooms are always good for grounding, earthly energy, as they spring directly from the soil.

SHIITAKE (*Lentinula edodes*)

What It Is

The shiitake is a popular edible and medicinal mushroom native to East Asia. They are small to medium in size—about four to eight inches (ten to twenty centimeters) in diameter—with wide, curled, umbrella-shaped caps that range from light to dark brown atop thin stems. Underneath the cap and not attached to the stem are white, tight gills that may be veiled depending on maturity. This species grows in clusters on dead hardwoods, like beech, maple, oak, and poplar.

How It's Used

The second most commonly consumed mushroom next to the button species, this type is incredibly popular in East Asian cuisine. Shiitakes are great for frying, sautéing, grilling, and boiling, releasing a garlic-pine aroma with savory, earthy, and smokey flavors. They are also known to be great dried and ground, used as a powdered flavoring. They are also said to have medicinal uses, known in Chinese traditional medicine to treat a cold, ward off hunger, and increase energy.

Magickal Properties

Because of the shiitake's versatility and flavoring, it is very aligned with healing and cleansing. Its coloring and aroma also lend to grounding and meditative applications, and additionally increase liveliness and vitality. Growing wild since ancient times and first cultivated during the Song dynasty between 960 and 1279 CE, this mushroom is also aligned with immortal metaphysical agents.

How to Use in Spells

Since this mushroom is so heavily used in culinary applications, it is a no-brainer to use it in kitchen witchcraft. Adding it to a stir-fry while stirring the ingredients counterclockwise can help bring in health, healing, and vitality. If you also include garlic and yuzu, you can increase this mushroom's cleansing and warding properties. Steeping this mushroom in tea while whispering an intention into the mug is another easy way to work magick with this mushroom.

POPULAR MEDICINAL MUSHROOMS

Lion's Mane (*Hericium erinaceus*)
Used traditionally in Eastern medicine, the lion's mane has a variety
of applications. Containing zinc, potassium, calcium, and beta-glucan
polysaccharides, this mushroom is excellent as a treatment for
inflammation that balances the human body, but it can also be used
topically. It is used to treat wounds by applying directly to the skin to
speed up the healing process. This mushroom is also excellent for the
mind and is said to reduce anxiety and improve memory. Use this in
spells for healing and intelligence.

Turkey Tail (*Trametes versicolor*)
These fungi grow on decomposing wood and are multicolored and
striped, hence their name. They contain B3 and D vitamins, which help to
boost the immune system, and also prebiotics that aid in digestion. They
also have antioxidants and antibacterial properties such as flavonoids
and phenols. They are known as *yunzhi* by traditional Chinese herbalists
and described as swirling clouds, consisting of the air element. They are
prescribed as a tea or medicinal drink to promote a long life, increase
energy and strength, and aid in digestion. Use this mushroom in spells
for both healing and transformation by brewing into a tea.

Reishi is used exclusively for its healing properties. It has a deep red, fanlike and kidney-shaped cap with no gills; instead, it releases spores through the fine pores existing on the underside. Containing beta-glucans, it is said to fight cancer cells. It is also known to lower blood pressure and prevent blood clotting. Like the other listed medicinal mushrooms, this mushroom is an anti-inflammatory. Used in traditional Chinese medicine, it is said to be made of *ling* (spirit) and *zhi* (plant) and is associated with longevity. Medicines using this fungus are generally prepared as a hot water extract, so one may use reishi for anointing themselves or others when concocting spells.

Chaga (*Inonotus obliquus*)

A parasitic fungus on trees such as birch, this nutrient-dense superfood contains antiaging antioxidants and is known to neutralize free radicals. It is also said that chaga can lower cholesterol and blood pressure, and the nutrients it contains are said to prevent cancer. It is recommended as a support to the immune system. Used for centuries in traditional Russian medicine, chaga is also found in northern Europe, Siberia, Korea, northern Canada, and Alaska. Traditionalists would brew this mushroom in tea to release its nutrients, so a practitioner may do the same to promote both healing and vitality.

Cordyceps

A genus rather than a species, this category of fungi is parasitic and grows on insect larvae. *Cordyceps* are used in traditional Chinese medicine to treat fatigue, sickness, kidney disease, and even low sex drive. Similar to the other organisms in this section, it can increase energy and is anti-inflammatory; a few scientific studies have said it aids in slowing the growth of tumors. One can ingest this supplement in pill form, and if using for spells in a morning ritual, one can simply consume it with the intention of strength, passion, and healing.

PART 2

Mushroom Folklore
Across the Globe

Maybe you've seen a psychedelic painting of a mushroom that glows in black light, or an adorable watercolor of one in a children's book. Whether illuminated in a college dorm or adorning a storybook, it's no secret that these fungi are associated with the nature-based fae. The traditional image of tiny fairies or elven folk situated atop brightly colored toadstool caps didn't just come out of thin air. All across Europe, we'll see associations between the fair folk and these complex organisms.

Mushrooms have been foraged across the globe from prehistoric times, and they have vastly different relationships with the cultures they intersect. As a seat of magickal life, delicious culinary item, or harbinger of death, the mushroom is a powerful symbol that can house a variety of meanings. This section will cover just a selection of them.

Most likely because of mushrooms' ability to grow from decaying wood or spring from the soil, there are many cultures that regard the fungi as a path to immortality. In addition, many ancient civilizations believe the mushroom to be a divine contribution across pantheons, and therefore see them as a way for humans to regain vitality, or even as a conduit for special powers. The fungi are honored not necessarily because of the way the mushroom looks (as we know looks can be deceptive,) but in the actual existence, life cycle, and gifts that mushrooms are.

One of the most interesting beliefs is the idea that mushrooms hover between planes of existence. Because of their perception as a liminal object, mushrooms are perfect symbols for divine presence on earth—a window into the heavens or the underworld. They exist between ugliness and beauty, decay and birth, death and immortality, and even feast or famine—mushroom iconography on every continent is situated carefully between realms.

It would also be a mistake to overlook the medicinal uses of mushrooms across the globe. Mushrooms were used to treat a variety of ailments in ancient China and in Russia from the thirteenth century to the present day; even now we see numerous new products that contain mushrooms for health benefits. This demonstrates not only the cultural importance of the mushroom, but its nutritional benefits as well. Even further, the widespread belief that these small growths of fungi can heal wounds, balance the body, and influence energy points to their significance, whether or not science can definitively demonstrate these results.

This section will show you the powerful importance of mushrooms from the perceived to the proven across many customs and traditions. By the end of this book, you shall have not only a repertoire from which to build your own belief system but also a vast understanding of the transformative identity of these incredible fungi.

EGYPT

Regarded by the pharaohs as "a gift from the God Osiris," mushrooms in ancient Egypt were reserved for royalty and kept far from the mouths of commoners who were not even allowed to touch the magickal fungi. Their association with Osiris is not only interesting but logical, as Osiris is the god of fertility, life, agriculture, vegetation, the afterlife, the dead, and resurrection. When we inspect the life-death cycle, we can see how the mushroom fits into the folklore of Osiris, as it is a fungus that springs to life out of decay. Because of this metaphysical belief, it was said that consuming mushrooms led to both immortality and the conception of supernatural powers. This belief dates back to at least 4500 BCE, when enchanted fungi were scrawled onto temple walls and on papyrus in hieroglyphics. Egypt is widely considered to be "the cradle of mycology," because not only were mushrooms found in Egyptian art and writing, but

they also appeared in architecture and jewelry. There are many temples, for example the Philae Temple, that house countless pillars resembling mushrooms. In terms of jewelry, the Hedjet, or white Egyptian crown of lower Egypt, and the Hemhem, the more elaborate version of the Adjet crown which was worn by the Pharaoh Tutankhamun, is adorned with mushroomlike ornamentations.

GREECE

As in ancient Egypt, where mushrooms were associated with the gods, in ancient Greece they also aligned mushrooms with their own mythology. The Eleusinian Mysteries were cult initiations held every year since mid-fourth century BCE spanning at least one thousand years, and were known as the most famous of the secret religious rites of ancient Greece. Linked to the short seasonal growth of morel mushrooms, the lore of Demeter and Persephone is directly correlated with the arrival of spring. When fair Persephone, a maiden archetype, was abducted by Hades and dragged to the underworld, her mother, Demeter, cursed the earth to not bear any vegetation until her daughter was returned. Zeus stepped in to facilitate a deal between the lord of the underworld and Demeter, and they reached an agreement that Persephone would come back to the earth each spring, when vegetation would begin again, but would live the majority of her days in the underworld. Because of this myth, the Eleusinian Mysteries held sacred rituals that cycled through the "descent," "the search," and the "ascent," using psychedelic mushrooms to achieve a sort of enlightenment and closeness to the goddesses. In pottery and paintings illustrating the different aspects of the Mysteries, both Demeter and Persephone are regularly depicted holding mushrooms. These rites were attended by some of Greece's most influential philosophers, including Socrates, Plato, and Aristotle, who were present for the various and complicated initiations that were centered around the transformation facilitated by psilocybin.

ROMAN EMPIRE

As with many other discoveries, the Romans looked to the Greeks for influence regarding mushrooms. Similar to both the ancient Egyptians and Greeks, the Romans deemed mushrooms a "food of the Gods," forbidding commoners from consuming the delicacy. However, noting the nutritional benefits and clear health advantages of the fungi, they allowed warriors to indulge in mushrooms before combat to ensure a victory. Because some Greek authors posited that mushrooms grew because Zeus flung their seeds to the earth via lightning bolts, the Romans surmised that thunderstorms were a vital ingredient to the growth of these fungi, as mushrooms did tend to spring up in clusters after rain. Interestingly, despite the alignment with mythological godheads, the Romans were less concerned about the ritual and magick of mushrooms and more about their practical applications in decadent feasts, food for soldiers, and, quite famously, poison. In 54 AD, Emperor Claudius was allegedly poisoned by the notorious Locusta, hired by his wife, Agrippina. Claudius was not popular in Rome, and his intended heir, Brittanicus, was a minor. Agrippina's son, Nero, was of age, and therefore a threat to this succession. So Agrippina took matters into her own hands by hiring a poisoner to feed her husband a feast of poisonous mushrooms to secure Nero's place on the throne. Aside from culinary and homicidal applications, it's notable that ancient Romans were instrumental in furthering scientific study on wild growth and cultivation of mushrooms.

MEXICO

In Central Mexico during the era of Aztec power, there were several gods who had associations with mushrooms. Piltzintecuhtli was the god of the rising sun, healing, and visions. Sometimes referred to as "seven flowers," he governed over hallucinatory plants, including mushrooms, which were very important in ritual ascendance. Xochipilli, the prince of flowers, and god of summer, pleasure, love, and dancing, is

regularly depicted as adorned with mushrooms and other hallucinogenics while sitting in a trancelike state. Because of the landscape of Central Mexico, a valley wedged between high mountains and deep canyons, mushrooms were quite difficult to procure, so foraging was considered a sacred practice. After fasting, the elite of Aztec culture would ingest the sacrament, *teonanácatl* (literally meaning "god mushroom"), by drinking chocolate or mezcal and adding honey to the fungi. This ritual, taking place at night, would lead the upper class to live freely by dancing, weeping, or sitting still and nodding. Unfortunately, after witnessing the ritual, Spanish settlers deemed the practice demonic and forced the practice underground.

FRANCE

France, particularly Paris, has a rich history when it comes to mushrooms. The City of Light is built upon local limestone that sits atop many tunnels, comprising a labyrinth of catacombs and an extensive underground history. The many cave-ins of the Holy Innocents' Cemetery in the late 1700s prompted six million bodies to be transferred to these tunnels, creating catacombs in which mushrooms would soon grow. King Louis XIV is said to be the first cultivator of the rare champignon de Paris mushroom. The so-called *rose de pres* (pink of the fields), which got its name from the mushroom's color, evolved to a shade like the limestone in which the mushrooms grew. This practice of cultivation was discovered by deserters of Napoleon's army, who lived underground, and noted that between the limestone, general environment, and horse's manure, the mushrooms had ideal conditions to grow year round.

IRELAND

There is a deep connection between the Emerald Isle and mushroom folklore dating back to the ancient Druids. Like other ancient civilizations, the Irish said mushrooms were the "flesh of the gods" and were consumed by the Druids for their psychoactive affects. Because both the liberty cap and fly agaric species are native to Ireland, they were used by Druids to reach transformation and enlightenment. But their significance doesn't end there. Halloween, or Samhain, has Celtic roots, and is said to be the night when the veil between the dead and the living is at its thinnest. It was custom to dress as animals and monsters to keep the evil spirits at bay, including mischievous fairies. Being that both liberty cap and fly agaric are naturally grown in the autumn months, it is believed that the Druids consumed these mushrooms to see the fairies they feared. Similarly, for other ritualistic rites, Druids would consume these mushrooms at other points in time before sitting in a sweat house to see elves, fae, and leprechauns, should they need enlightenment. In Gaelic slang, mushrooms and fairies share the same word: *pookies*.

GERMANY AND AUSTRIA

Germany and Austria have similar mushroom lore, given their geographical proximity to each other, although they differ greatly from other regions of Europe. While mushrooms are tied to water and fertilization in many cultures, in German and Austrian customs they are more closely tied to fire and cleansing. For example, a huge part of mushroom mythology lies in "fairy rings," which are circular or patterned clusters of mushrooms said to hold quite a bit of magick. Science describes this phenomenon as a mushroom spore falling in a favorable spot, creating an underground tubular network called a *hyphae*, with mushroom caps appearing above the surface in the shape of a ring. In Germany and Austria,

this phenomenon has long carried sinister implications. In Austria, a Tyrolean legend explains the fairy ring as having been burned into the ground by the fiery tail of dragons. In Germany, it is called a *Hexenringe*, or witches ring, within which witches would dance on Walpurgis Night. Germany also ties mushrooms to Christmas and New Year's, although in this context the Germans reference the fly agaric and deem it a good luck charm. The *glücklicher Pilz*, or lucky mushroom, is used to adorn wreaths, and is also said to be a gift from the *Schornsteinfeger*, or chimney sweep, who comes to cleanse the hearth on New Year's Eve. You can see this depiction in many pieces of Eastern European art.

ENGLAND

Dwellers on this isle in western Europe tend to see mushrooms as much less ominous than their neighbors to the east. In England, fairy rings are simply a place where the fair folk dance and where sprites can sit atop the caps of toadstools to rest in between festivities. However, mischievous and territorial folk that fairies are, it is said that, upon entrance into the ring, a human may be transported to fairyland

never to return. If a human were to stumble upon a fairy dance and try to join, she would be forced to dance until she passed out from exhaustion, as this festivity sometimes lasts for days on end. In some more dire cases, entrance to a fairy ring might lead to an early death. In the British Isles, farmers warned that the grass inside the rings was poisonous and dis-ease causing to any animal that crossed its path. Shakespeare even wrote about fairy rings in *The Tempest*, warning, "Whereof the ewe not bites, and you whose pastime is to make midnight mushrooms. . . ." However, the lore suggests that an animal can be cured after eating this grass if they consume St. John's wort harvested at midnight on St. John's night. Additionally, like the Druids of Ireland, Druids in Stonehenge were said in ancient tales to practice magick and ascendance by consuming the iconic fly agaric mushroom.

RUSSIA

The Baba Yaga is an important figure in Russian mythology. Babas, or older women, generally carried the role of healers, and Baba Yaga is no different. As a healer, she is sometimes pictured with mushrooms, which is not surprising. Baba Yaga is mainly seen with the fly agaric, which decorates her home in the woods. She is so grotesque that she emanates a sort of beauty—she isn't quite evil, neither is she good, and she straddles the line between life and death, both by her neutrally heroic efforts in some lore and objective cursing in others. The Leshii, on the other hand, was a demon-god who sought to protect the creatures of the forest. Known as a trickster, quite similar to a fairy, this tree spirit was known to transform into many different forms. Outside the forest he was synonymous with the devil. Yet inside the woods, he could lead peasants astray by disguising himself as a person, beast, animal, or, of course, a mushroom. Once foraged as a mushroom, he would either make unlucky peasants sick when consumed or tickle them to death when portraying a hominid, which is an odd but apt metaphor for poisonous mushrooms.

RUSSIA (SIBERIA)

The myth of Santa Claus has many, many different sources. In Siberia, however, this festive, jolly harbinger of presents and joy has a slightly different appearance and personality. Up until a few hundred years ago, shamans in this region would consume fly agaric mushrooms to commune with the spirit world. Come late December, they would forage for the fly agaric and dry them, then enter locals' homes to leave them as gifts on the winter solstice for the locals to indulge in. In the Northern Hemisphere, fly agaric mushrooms grow naturally under conifers and birch trees, and because they appear red with white dots, they are reminiscent of wrapped presents under a tree. Another local technique was to dry these mushrooms and hang them from tree branches, much like ornaments, leading to the Christmas tradition with which many of us are familiar. Another interesting connection is that, like the shamans (and sometimes the residents), the indigenous reindeer of the Northern Hemisphere also ingested the fly agaric mushroom, making them behave erratically. It is suggested that, when hallucinating, the locals may have believed the reindeer to fly. Rudolph's nose has been correlated with the ability of the mushroom to lead the way during "flight."

CHINA

The Chinese favor two mushrooms specifically in their lore and mythology: the lingzhi and shiitake. With a flat cap of red to yellow to white that almost looks like a sunburst, the lingzhi, which we'll cover first, has a strong spiritual association in Chinese

history. It is said that if you find a lingzhi mushroom wild, it can bene-fit your enlightenment more than any other herb available. One legend goes that a driven student, aptly named Mr. Ambition, studied in his small Chinese village to pass the exams required to be a government offi-cial. However, when he continued to fail the exams, he shifted his "ambi-tion" to being a Taoist monk, living in a temple on the mountain and only eating vegetables. One day, he caught a glimpse of his reflection and was frightened to see that he looked ill. At this point, he believed being a monk was no longer for him and returned back to his village, where he began work in construction. After laboring some time in building up the village, he and his crew found a strange object, and Mr. Ambition pondered if this was a bad omen for him. Still looking sickly, he brought the item to a local fortune-teller, who told him that this item would bring negativity to his life unless he were to eat it that evening. Magickally, once consumed, Mr. Ambition started to regain life in his body. Later that week, a Taoist monk passed by his construction site and noticed Mr. Ambition. The monk asked to take him aside, and inquired if he'd eaten anything strange. After talking with him for some time, the monk determined that Mr. Ambition had eaten the lingzhi and had become immortal. The two went back to the temple on the mountain, where Mr. Ambition still lives.

As for the shiitake, which is known in China as *shanku* and *dongo*, it too has a divine origin. It is said that a deity named Shennong bestowed the world with natural treasures, including medicinal mushrooms, which are hugely important in Eastern medicine. The shiitake is still used today as an aphrodisiac and promoter of youthfulness, with its roots in Shennong's largesse.

JAPAN

As in China, mushroom lore in Japan is dominated by associations with the shiitake mushroom. While Chinese tales routinely have foragers finding the fungi in the wild, Japanese stories often reflect their early cultivation methods: by cutting a log, placing it horizontally, and injecting it with spores in a moist atmosphere, mushrooms were grown and harvested. This is called the "stroke and strike" method, and in Japanese culture it is often used as a metaphor for a boy evolving into a man. Inoculated logs were passed down by family members, and the men would keep them as inherited "fortune." Japan knows the mushroom, referred to as lingzhi in China, as reishi, a mushroom that was recognized as traditional Taoist medicine in 1400 CE. It has been depicted in many art forms including jewelry, furniture, and paintings, an acknowledgment of its significance as a healing property.

The Japanese name many different species of mushrooms after animals, colors, or even belief systems. *Kinoko*, the word for mushroom, quite literally means "child of the tree"; the mushroom is considered to be an organism that exists between the plant and animal world. Farmers highly regard thunderstorms, believing them to be gifts from the divine. It is said that when lightning strikes into the earth, mushrooms will grow, creating a bridge between heaven and earth. Because the mushroom produces oxygen, creates relationships with its source of food, and is food itself, the boundless ability of this organism can be seen as otherworldly. It is because of its fluid existence that it is so treasured, and why it is seen as magickal and immortal. Aside from the ancient implication of power and importance, the mushroom is also *kawaii*, or cute, which brings its symbology into modern cultural importance via the likes of the company Sanrio or the artist Takashi Murakami.

KOREA

Mushrooms are central to a variety of Korean practices. In Korean, the shiitake is called *pyogo* and is used as an ingredient in many dishes. But the *pyogo* is far from the only mushroom of importance. For example, in 2018, North Korea sent a shipment of two tons of pine mushrooms to South Korea. Beyond their culinary importance, this shipment was meant to honor the families of those that could not attend an inter-Korean summit, one of the first between North and South Korea. The mushrooms were to be distributed to over four thousand families from Pyongyang to Seoul. Pine mushrooms may be an important regional product, featured on stamps and other products, but their importance runs deeper. Surprisingly, these mushrooms have been used as a sort of currency in North Korea. The North Korean government will collect mushrooms from residents in exchange for daily necessities.

In ancient Korean mythology, the fungi make an appearance as both a symbol of punishment and good fortune. In the tale, Gameunjang-aegi, goddess of destiny, was the third child of two beggar parents. After her birth, the parents became wealthy, and when asking each daughter why they had such good fortune, Gameunjang-aegi credits herself and is cast away. Upon being confronted by her jealous and resentful older sisters, she turns one of them into a centipede and the other into a mushroom. She then leaves her home and meets her soon-to-be husband, who tends a land of silver and gold. After they marry,

Gameunjang-aegi discovers her parents have lost all of their wealth and become blind. Hoping to see them again, she hosts a feast for all of the beggars in the land. One by one, she feeds everyone a meal until she discovers her mother and father. After she serves them both, she reveals her identity, both restoring their sight and her sisters' natural forms. So, in this instance, the mushroom is used as a punitive measure: a lowly organism that can seem insignificant if not approached with care and respect.

INDIA

In ancient India, sacred offerings of the Vedic sacrifices were known as *somas*, named after the god of religious sacrifices for good fortune and, in some texts, the moon. One interpretation of a soma is based on a mushroom containing a derivative of the active ingredient found in the fly agaric. This compound was produced by simply placing the mushroom in between two rocks to squeeze out the juices, which were then filtered through sheep's wool and mixed with milk and water, as well as other ingredients. Once offered to the gods, the priests and sacrificer would sip the soma mixture to ascend to the heavens, aided by its hallucinogenic properties.

Legend says that the soma was locked in a heavenly citadel by an archer, then brought back to the earth by a falcon. This falcon presented soma to the first sacrificer as fertilizing rain, which brings forth all life. The process of pressing the fly agaric to create soma is thought to imitate the idea of generating rain and has also been used in other metaphors: a king conquering territory, the sun transiting astrologically, or a bull running to mate. In post-Vedic history, it is said that any consumers of soma are purified and cleansed of their sins and will attain a divine life in the heavens.

IRAN

Similar to Soma worship in India, ancient Persians also imbibed the sacred juice of mushrooms, known in this region as *haoma*. The Avesta, a written account of the oral history passed down through generations, includes a four-thousand-year-old reference to when the sacrament used in religious ceremonies was ultimately replaced with a nonpsychoactive ingredient. The ritual in question was called *yasna*, the principal act of worship in Zoroastrianism, and it is still performed today, albeit without the influence of mushrooms. The *yasna* deals with the battle between order and chaos. Participants present fire, the meat from a sacrificial animal, and haoma as offerings, which are said to

bridge the gap between human and the divine in the spirit of the holy order. The purpose of this offering is to give power to deities so they may impose love and good fortune among the people of the land and prevent the cosmos from falling into disorder.

TIBET/NEPAL

As with the ritualistic drinks imbibed above, Tibetan monks were known to indulge in an elixir called *amrita* to aid in the spiritual experience. It would not be surprising that, given the name, it is a derivative of *Amanita muscaria*, or the fly agaric, which so many ancients around the globe were known to love. It is said that the large, radiating crown behind Buddha's head depicted in most art symbolizes the cap of this mushroom when turned on its side. While, yes, it is part of the vow of Buddhists to not drink or do drugs, the natural substance was held, as in most cultures, to be a sacred tool for enlightenment. This may be because it is said that Buddha died of dysentery after eating a poisonous mushroom (or spoiled pork, in some texts). And while that may seem the opposite of holy, the story goes as such: One of Buddha's followers offered him a meal as an offering while visiting his mango grove. Shortly after, Buddha died of fatal dysentery between two trees. Before making his way to nirvana, he asked one of his disciples to visit this follower and tell him not to worry, for he did not kill Buddha, but rather allowed him to ascend via his last meal, turning decay into salvation.

MALAYSIA

The lore behind the tiger milk mushroom, hailed as Malaysia's national treasure, speaks of its rarity. As this particular mushroom sprouts singularly, instead of in a cluster, it is very hard to find. It is said that the fungus springs up where a tigress has spilled her milk when feeding her cubs, leading to its name. The sclerotium, or hard resting body of the mushroom, is described as looking like a glass of old milk, again leading to the myth. Because of its rarity and fabled origin, it is said to have healing and life-giving properties. The Semai, indigenous Malaysians, believe that it has the ability to bring life into a crop, which will lead to a bountiful harvest. Other native tribes aligned it with the soul of a tiger cub and associated it with healthy child birth. Most of the Malaysian origins of the tiger milk mushroom state this fungus is more visible after the full moon, and it is still sought after today.

PHILIPPINES

The indigenous tribes of the mountains of the ancient Philippines have many theories about how the world was created, but the most appropriate for this section is the Manobo cosmogony myth from upper Agusan people. The Agusan believe that the earth is shaped like a giant mushroom with its stem erect out of the core, and deities shake this stem vigorously when angered by the humans below. This makes sense when considering the many earthquakes that occur in the Philippines, but also again aligns the symbology of mushrooms with heavens and earth, chaos and order, and life and death. Another piece of popular mushroom lore in the Philippines exists within the beds of mushrooms that lay upon mounds of earth. These mushrooms are the home of the *duwende*, or dwarf. It is said that if people, often children in cautionary tales, step on the duwende, they must be very polite and say "excuse me" and beg for forgiveness. However, if they make it angry or harm it in any way, the duwende will curse them and spit on them, resulting in a fatal condition that only a faith healer can remedy.

THAILAND

Turning to spookier mythology—really more of a tale of a cryptid than a myth, given that these creatures are based on twenty-first-century sightings—the Krasue is an interesting mix of feminism and gore. The story goes that a princess was sent to burn at the stake by her jealous husband, who accused her of having an affair with a lowly soldier. As the princess began to suffer in the flames, a witch happened to pass by and promised to return her to life with a black magick spell. However, because the spell revived the princess a little too late, only her unburnt remains were necromanced: her head and viscera. Now the Krasue, ever gluttonous, is known to roam the forests and villages at night as simply a head with glowing organs spilling from her throat, where she feasts on raw flesh and blood. Only active at night, the Krasue joins the ghost of her body during the day to roam like a zombie, sullen and somber. But once the night falls, she feasts on anything from cattle to newborns to unsuspecting villagers. Although many protect themselves from this entity with spiked fences, it is said that to kill a Krasue, one must destroy her head-less body so that the apparition can never rejoin the neck. The feminist aspect of the myth is quite clear in the disembodiment and demoniz-ing of the female sprit, but what of the mushrooms? In terms of this tale, it is said that one of the approximately 600 biolumi-nescent species of mushrooms that natively grows in Khon Kaen is named the Krasue mushroom, and it is said to illuminate when a Krasue passes by. It is unknown if this particular species is hallucinogenic, but it may contribute to the sightings if so.

NIGERIA

There are many wonderful pieces of folklore surrounding mushrooms in Yoruban culture. One story is about a woman named Oran who is desperate to give birth but cannot conceive. Seeking consultation, Oran visits an *Orunmila*, or a wise man who is a sanctioned deputy on the earth for God, or Olodumare. The Orunmila instructs Oran to make a sacrifice and gives her a list of all the necessary ingredients: sixteen chameleons, sixteen fowls, and however many maize grains would equal the number of her desired children. But in her haste, Oran forgets to retrieve the fowls. She gathers her supplies and gives them to the Orunmila, who prepares a concoction for her to drink, and further instructs her to use a white cloth when she begins to deliver her children. Immediately after drinking Orunmila's brew, Oran begins to give birth, and what springs forth are a species of agaric mushroom. The Yoruban people believe that when this mushroom first emerges from the ground, it will take the shape of the person it sees first. So if the passerby is tall and lean, the mushroom will be tall and lean. This association is because of the sixteen chameleons given in sacrifice by Oran. This particular mushroom also grows in large groups, which is linked to the large number of maize grains in the Orunmila's list of ingredients. Because of their white caps, when spotted from above, they resemble the *Termitomyces microcarpus*, white sheet. However, because of the missing ingredient, it is said that her offspring was soon discovered to be edible by man, and thus her children were to be eaten for all eternity.

Another myth surrounding the *T. robustus* is about a man named Ogogo, who visits an Orunmila to remove his own bad luck. Upon following all of the Orunmila's instructions on ingredients to gather, Ogogo and the Orunmila go to a nearby tree, where the Orunmila washes Ogogo's head in seven places around the tree trunk. He instructs Ogogo to return with him in nine days. When they return after nine days have passed, they discover that mushrooms have grown in each of the seven spots where Ogogo had his head washed, and the Orunmila rejoices that Ogogo's luck has been restored. This mushroom varietal is known as a bestower of abundance because of this tale.

CONGO

Originating in the Congo region, a *nkisi* is an object that is meant to be inhabited by a spirit. The nkisi carries a great deal of importance because of its ability to protect its bearer, as well as its symbolic role as a seat of the divine. Healers, diviners, and ceremonialists would create *minkisi* (the plural identifier) to guard against those who sought to do them harm. Because the healers that created minkisi communed with many ancestors and gods, they would invoke these spirits to place inside the nkisi. One of the most favorable vessels that could become a nkisi was, in fact, the mushroom. This is because of a few different factors: for one, the color of the mushroom in that region was usually white, symbolic of purity, but also the passage to the spirit world. Also, as a fungus, it bridged life and death. Finally, if a toxic mushroom became a nkisi, it was thought to be especially aggressive in its protection against harm. Associated with the elements, there are two types of minkisi: those of the above (sky, rain, and thunderstorms—all thought to lead to mushrooms) and of the below, or the earth, again associated with the fungi. It is also no surprise that when abducted into the slave trade, many Africans of this region tried to smuggle their minkisi in order to protect themselves from their captors.

MADAGASCAR

According to popular belief among anthropologists, the Vazimba people were the first inhabitants of Madagascar. Whether they are indigenous or immigrants, historical or fabled, they are a source of interest in African history. Between archaeological research and oral history, it has been gathered that these people, upon arrival, mainly foraged for food, aside from occasionally hunting small game. As their population grew in size, the Vazimba separated into villages that retained a hierarchy, first with chiefs at the top, and later kings. The most noble among these rulers would distinguish themselves by dying their hair red, which was done by soaking it in a mixture incorporating the local mushroom species. To the Vazimba, red was a symbol of power and the spirit of a warrior. However, in modern-day Madagascar, it is thought that these people never existed at all and are actually monsters that haunt the land they were said to have inhabited. In fact, these creatures are described as looking quite similar to mushrooms, either being very pale or very dark, small in stature, and unable to come into contact with salt, which will drastically dehydrate them. Similarly, the Vazimba were said to submerge their dead in water, and if we know anything about mushrooms to this point, we know mushrooms love decay and moisture.

PERU

Mushrooms can be found in ancient Peruvian art forms as far back as 1200 BCE and up until 1532 CE. There's no secret that the mushroom was an integral part of artistic expression for the Peruvians and that it also carried spiritual significance. In the Cupisnique culture, the oldest of the coastal civilizations in Peru, you'll often see mushrooms depicted in a tree of life formation on vessels for drinking, alongside feline images and decapitated heads. This symbolism is beautiful—the mushrooms are the bridge between the mythical and the mortal, sitting between feline familiars and shamans as well as dramatic symbols of death.

The Paracas culture of the coast featured mushrooms on textiles and ceramics alongside shamans who were either in flight or battle. As the myth goes, mushrooms gave shamans the ability to "fly" because of their hallucinogenic properties, but they also facilitated entrance into the spirit world, where, at times, a shaman may be called to fight in order to gain enlightenment or heal illness.

The Moche society created ceramics depicting mushrooms adorning a *curandero*, or healer, on the top of the head, some specifically with unmistakable fly agaric imagery. The Chimu culture focused more heavily on the tumi, however, which does predate their culture, but is used as more popular iconography in their art forms. This religious sacrificial knife, which in modern day has many practical uses, has a mushroom-shaped base, and in this particular culture is often ornamented with more mushrooms along the shaft and head of the piece.

In the highland areas, the Pukara culture, the oldest of this region, created decorations similar to the Cupisnique's, but their use of the mushroom is a little more direct. Pukara vases depict a large-eyed feline, its trance state indicated with mushroom-capped ears. This culture also produced mushroom-shaped stones, quite similar to those at Lake Titicaca in Chucuito, which is the subject of much controversy. Historians have long argued about whether they are phallic in nature or mushroom shaped. Either way, they both bring about life.

VENEZUELA/COLOMBIA

Women, beware in this region during the rainy season, for the Kayeri may cross your path. This mythical creature is said to live below the mushrooms during rainy season, springing to life in a humanoid shape and shouting the only word it can speak, "*Mu, mu, mu!*" while banging on trees. Legend goes that when the soil is dry, Kayeri stays underground to hibernate, using the holes of anthills for air. However, after fresh rain falls, the Kayeri emerges, using each mushroom as a cap. Incredibly fast and strong, the Kayeri feeds primarily on cows, eating the animal whole, hooves and all. However, as bigamists, with two wives each, they do enjoy human females. These creatures are known to enchant females lost on their land to inflict all sorts of evil, and the only known way to kill one is by striking it in the kidneys with a bone-tipped arrow. One story goes that a hunter's two daughters were abducted by a Kayeri, and after the hunter shot him in the kidneys, the monster turned into a pebble so the hunter could flee without harm. As they ran away, all they could hear in the distance was the boom of trees being struck with a shriek of "*Mu, mu, MU!*"

UNITED STATES

Haploporus odorus has an obvious characteristic, given its Latin name—it's known for its fragrance. Used by the Northern Plains indigenous peoples, including the Dakota, the Nakota, and the Lakota, as a decorative symbol on sacred objects, it was also known as a healing tool. Not only was the *H. Odorus* used topically to treat wounds and ingested to treat dysentery, but it was also symbolic of power and prestige, used to adorn robes and headdresses of revered warriors. It was worn on jewelry to protect against illness, as well as placed in medicine bags. It would also be burned to produce a healing, perfumed smoke, and carved and burnt as an adornment or offering. The uses listed above are indicative of the fluidity of the mushroom's power.

Over on the northwest coast, *Fomitopsis officinalis* duped a group of anthropologists who originally thought the carvings they discovered were made from wood; much to their surprise, they were made from the fruiting bodies of this native mushroom. The carvings they'd found were placed at the graves of shamans, letting unwanted spirits know the grave was well protected.

AUSTRALIA

Similar to the tale of the Krasue, the bioluminescent mushrooms of aboriginal Australia carry an ominous aura. Said to be associated with meteors, which in turn brought serpents, evil magick, and even death, the glowing mushrooms were feared by aboriginals, who wouldn't touch them and referred to them as "ghost mushrooms." When aboriginals saw these mushrooms, they would cry "spirit!" and step quickly away. Since the "ghost mushrooms" were thought to have come from a meteor, they were believed to be an omen of a spirit who was returning unwelcomed to the world of the living. This fear stems even more deeply from the energy carried by the meteor, a dark magick called *Arungquilta*, which was harnessed in a ceremony to cast punishment, likely death, on those that broke a taboo. So, it's no mystery as to why Australian aboriginals were afraid of the glowing fungi.

PART 3

Spellcasting with Fungi

When you know the energetic correspondences of the ingredients you use, you can enhance your magick with any kind of mushroom, whether store-bought or those you've foraged yourself. Again, I must stress that an expert should oversee wild mushroom foraging. In addition, seeking out a knowledgeable forager in order to source wild mushrooms can have a great educational impact on your practice, and it can inform new intentions down the line.

This section is not the be-all-end-all of mushroom magick, but rather a suggestion of how to build your own spells around them. By using color magick, or the use of energetic attachment to the hues found in your ingredients, cultural links, and metaphysical correspondences, this section will give you examples of how to use common fungi to manifest, hex, and heal.

Alternatives to listed mushrooms will be given, and feel free to substitute types of mushrooms or other ingredients where you may feel it is necessary. All spells mentioned in this section will reference the mushrooms identified in this guide, specifically.

Whether you have just begun your witchcraft practice or are simply looking to add a new tool to your repertoire, this section is fluid enough for you to customize to your liking.

You will gain a small overview of how each spell will work, suggested mushrooms, and example instructions for you to implement. The only caution necessary is that you should beware of poisonous fungi—please make sure your tools are the correct variant of mushrooms so that you do not harm yourself. Again, seek out an expert when foraging or using wild mushrooms.

MONEY

Money spells are pretty self-explanatory, as they are performed to bring more money into one's life. However, there are a few misconceptions about this type of spellwork. For one, as with all witchcraft, compensation requires action. Wishing for more money while sitting on the couch is asking the universe for a bit too much, so there must be some give and take. Perhaps you'd like more money in the form of a promotion, or you're launching a product and need energetic help to make it a success. Those are appropriate and successful uses of money spells.

How Can Mushrooms Help?

Luckily, many of the mushrooms discussed in the first section of this book that are associated with abundance are edible, which means you can literally put your money where your mouth is. By ingesting an abundant ingredient, you can feel its effects from the inside out. Working specifically with the chakra system, a Vedic ideology mapping sources of energy throughout the body, we see that the heart chakra is green. When we imagine food flowing through our chest with a green glow attached to it, the color of money, we can literally imbibe our financial goals.

What You Need

Pan to sauté

Ingredients

3 tablespoons olive oil

16 ounces cremini mushrooms
(also known as baby bella)

$^1/_4$ cup fresh rosemary

$^1/_4$ cup fresh basil

Salt and pepper to taste

Half a lemon

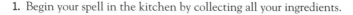

Spell Instructions

1. Begin your spell in the kitchen by collecting all your ingredients.

2. Before turning on the heat, make sure your ingredients are thoroughly washed and cleaned.

3. With all of your ingredients before you, begin to ground yourself by performing a body scan. Start from the top of your head, and imagine a white light glowing from your crown and enveloping your body inch by inch, protecting you while you work. Allow the light to spread over your ingredients and the area in which you are working.

4. Add your olive oil to the pan, asking it for balance, and turn your stove to medium heat.

5. Add your mushrooms, stating your intention to raise money specifically, whether it be by naming the amount, asking for a raise, and so on.

6. Stir clockwise for two minutes.

7. Add your herbs, asking for good fortune and blessings.

8. Add salt, asking for protection and purity.

9. Add pepper, asking for courage and motivation.

10. Stir clockwise for another four to five minutes, continuing to bring in abundance.

11. Once most of the liquid in the mushrooms has been cooked out, lower the heat and squeeze your lemon over the dish, asking for no harm done in receipt of your good fortune.

12. Thank the energies at play, and release the white light you gathered at the beginning of the spell into the universe.

13. Plate your dish (or side dish), and while eating, envision a green light flowing from your heart. Your spell is complete.

Other Variations

If cremini mushrooms are not at your disposal (though they are available at most grocery stores), you may also substitute black trumpet, hen of the woods, or porcini. All are edible and aligned with abundance; however, they will vary in taste. If mushrooms are not appetizing to you, feel free to dry and hang any of these varieties in your kitchen, create a money oil, a magickal satchel, or even a spell jar. Examples of all of these are listed in different ways throughout this section.

LOVE

Love spells, like money spells, have a somewhat negative connotation. Depending on the practice, some may feel that love spells must come with a sacrifice, specifically of the chosen target's free will. However, as I'm sure we can all agree, no relationship should start with a hostage situation—consent is always mandatory. Instead, increasing your amorous magnetism will help to attract the perfect mate rather than binding an unwilling participant to your energy. You can amplify this vibe by performing some simple candle magick, dressing your candle with homemade mushroom oil. While I've chosen to use this type of invocation

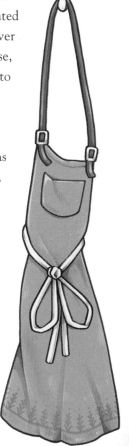

for the purposes of enhancing romantic attraction, it should be noted that money and love spellworkings are interchangeable, as they both are associated with the aforementioned heart chakra. So, however you choose to thrust the energy into the universe, you, the practitioner, should perform according to your intuition.

How Can Mushrooms Help?

Whether mushrooms across ancient civilizations have been aligned with vitality, immortality, abundance, or fertility, these cultural associations all circle back to the idea of romance. Why do we need energy and strength? To perform duties that may attract a mate. Why do we desire youth? To be irresistible to a mate. Why do we want money? To provide for a mate. Why would we desire fertility? To produce for a mate. And again, while the lifelong search for a mate is an archaic idea of what love and romance should be in the modern era, there's no denying that this simplistic view of energy alignment still carries weight in spellwork.

Things You Need

Baking sheet

Blender or food processor

Pot

Cheesecloth, 4 layers

Bowl

Clean jar

Pink chime or taper candle

Carving instrument

Lighter

Ingredients

Chanterelle mushrooms

1 cup olive oil

Bay leaf

Spell Instructions

1. Before you begin your spell, you will be creating an oil to dress your candle, although this can also be used for food in the future.

2. Begin by laying your mushrooms on a baking sheet in a single layer.

3. Dry these mushrooms at 150 degrees for approximately an hour.

4. Flip the mushrooms over, and continue to cook for another hour.

5. Remove and let cool.

6. Once you've dried your mushrooms, place them in a blender (or food processor) and blend until fine.

7. Pour the oil into a pot while asking for balance.

8. Drop in the mushrooms, asking for pure love.

9. Place the bay leaf into the pot, and ask for the manifestation of your desires.

10. Add heat, and ask for a quick return on your efforts. Let the mixture cook until it bubbles, carefully letting it boil for ten to fifteen seconds before removing from the heat.

11. Swirl until the mixture cools from boiling hot to warm.

12. Strain through the four layers of cheesecloth into your bowl, then transfer to your jar. Refrigerate for safekeeping.

13. Now that your oil is finished, you are ready to begin your spell. Start by grounding on the floor with your candle, oil, and carving tool before you. You can ground by envisioning roots growing from where your body touches the floor into the center of the earth. This will anchor you as you cast your spell.

14. After grounding, meditate on your intention. Perhaps it is to bring in your soulmate, a new date, or clarity on a current relationship. Hold this intention in your mind's eye.

15. Once you have your intention, pick a key word to symbolize your desire.

16. Use your carving tool to etch your key word into your candle.

17. Use your hands to coat the candle with the infused oil from the top to the middle and the bottom to the middle to "bring in" your intention.

18. Light your candle, and meditate on the flame while envisioning your intention.

19. When you feel ready, envision the roots that have anchored you growing back into your body, releasing you from the spell.

20. Put your candle somewhere safe, and let it burn all the way down. Your spell is complete.

Other Variations

If you cannot source chanterelle mushrooms, some excellent substitutes are beech, porcini, and shiitake, which are all edible. If candle magick is not aligned with your practice, feel free to substitute your intention into a recipe, satchel, or spell jar, depending on your preference.

HEXING

A hex, quite frankly, is energetic self-defense. The philosophy behind a hex is similar to martial arts combat: recommended to be used only when absolutely necessary. However, the ability to hex can be incredibly empowering—hexes have long been used by marginalized people to protect themselves from oppression. It is important that practitioners understand their own moral baseline, within which they may decide to hex. If practitioners decide to pursue the use of baneful magick, they must proceed with caution, at the very least. While not a necessary practice to engage in if you wish to identify as a witch, baneful magick is an important piece of witchcraft that is easily strengthened by mycological influence.

How Can Mushrooms Help?

Many different mushroom species are perfect for hexing. Because most energetic correspondences can be derived from the biological nature of an ingredient coupled with its historical use, it's easy to see how various fungi can be helpful when working a hex. Toxic varietals carry echoes of the poison they carry, sending a negative energy to your target. Parasitic species, which feed off their host, will have a draining effect. However, again, when engaging in a hexing, witches must take stock of their moral baseline before sending harm in anyone's way.

What You Need

Black marker

Slip of paper

Jar

A place to bury

Ingredients

Table salt

White vinegar

King trumpet mushroom

Spell Instructions

1. Begin your spell by centering yourself and asking if your subject is worthy of a hex. If you unequivocally decide yes, beyond a reasonable doubt, then that is your prerogative. But do devote some time to giving this practice some major thought.

2. Take your table salt and create a circle, starting clockwise from the northernmost position. Make sure your equipment is with you within the circle before casting, as you must not move outside of the circle once you begin.

3. Once your circle is created, ground into yourself by envisioning a white light emanating from the salt and illuminating all of your objects. Sit with this light for as long as feels comfortable.

4. Take your black marker and mark down your target's name on your slip of paper. Place it in the jar.

5. Pour the white vinegar into the jar and fill about halfway, concentrating on your target.

6. Place your king trumpet mushroom into the jar, asking it to remove this person's harm from your life.

7. Seal your jar, and shake it aggressively, focusing on your target.

8. Once finished, take the white light that you first focused on and send it up into the universe, asking for your hand to be clean and that your working was of the highest good.

9. Sweep up your salt in a counterclockwise motion.

10. Bury the jar in a safe place away from your property, and cease communication with your subject.

Other Variations

Hexing is a very powerful form of spellwork, so again, make sure your target is deserving of this hex. Suggested above for use is the king trumpet mushroom, a parasitic mushroom that feeds off its host yet is easily found in markets and is nontoxic for consumption. If foraged, or if one were to fall into your lap, a toxic mushroom like black saddle, honey agaric, or green amanita will also work as substitutes, but do not attempt contact with these varieties unless you are under direct consultation with an expert.

DIVINATION

Divination is the practice of using a tool to find answers to questions that your own intuition cannot answer. Some common methods of divination are reading tarot or runes and scrying. While there are a variety of other well-known tools out there, what may be more of a surprise is that you can divine with just about anything. Asking a question while meditating and shuffling a music playlist can provide a message. Flipping through a book while asking a question and landing on whichever page calls to you can also provide guidance. The Greeks and Turks practice tasseography and cafeomancy, the process of reading leftover tea leaves or coffee grounds, respectively.

How Can Mushrooms Help?

Because mushrooms can be dried, they can easily be used to create a tea that can be used for tasseography, or tea leaf reading. If you desire—depending on the kind of question for which you are seeking guidance (for example, love, business, or health)—you may choose to amplify the energy of your reading with an aligned mushroom. To choose the right variety, refer back to the first section of this book to choose a mushroom that is nontoxic and good for drying, and ideally has an alignment with the theme of your question.

What You Need

Baking sheet

Tea bag

Mug

Ingredients

White button mushrooms

1 tablespoon dried rose hips

1 tablespoon dried mugwort

Hot water

Honey, to taste

Lemon, to taste

Spell Instructions

1. Before you begin your spell, dry your white button mushrooms—you'll need enough to fill a single tea bag, but if you have more than you need, they're great to have on hand for cooking.

2. Begin by laying your mushrooms on a baking sheet in a single layer.

3. Dry these mushrooms at 150 degrees for approximately an hour.

4. Flip the mushrooms over, and continue to cook for another hour.

5. Take equal parts mushrooms, rose hips, and mugwort and place into your tea bag.

6. Heat water, pour into your mug, and add your tea bag.

7. Add honey to sweeten your answer and lemon to purify the response.

8. Before divining, whisper your question into the mug while the tea cools. You may stir clockwise as you whisper to help bring in your intention.

9. Drink your tea while you hold your intention in your mind's eye. When the tea is about three-quarters of the way finished, empty the contents of your bag into your mug and finish as much of the liquid as you can. Allow the solid particles to settle on the bottom of the mug.

10. From here, try to make out any symbols, characters, or letters your tea has created. This detritus holds the story of your answer. It is up to you to interpret it!

Other Variations

Any edible mushroom can be dried for consumption as tea. It is mostly common to make tea from meatier mushrooms such as chaga and reishi, which can be store-bought dried to bypass the process, but button mushrooms have a direct link to divination, and the process of drying brings the practitioner closer to the spell. One may also prefer to use an aligned mushroom with an energy that corresponds to money or love if their question revolves around that category. Just be certain the mushrooms you use are nontoxic.

CLEANSING

Cleansing spells are extremely useful for a myriad of reasons. Perhaps someone entered your home with a chaotic energy, or you've been in an overwhelming social environment, or you may even have had a bout of bad luck that you'd like to get past. Cleansing spells can help to rid these negative vibrations. While it may be in vogue to use sage or otherwise "clear the air" with smoke, there are a variety of other ways to tidy up your energetic field. Think of cleansing as spiritual maintenance; these kinds of spells can be incorporated into your monthly or weekly routine.

How Can Mushrooms Help?

There are three primary ways in which mushrooms are great for cleansing. First, mushrooms are known to have antibacterial and antifungal properties that cleanse the blood and body. These medicinal effects are cleansing on their own. Additionally, certain species of mushrooms, like oyster mushrooms, are known to actually cleanse the air of the environment they belong to. And finally, because mushrooms are so incredibly versatile, one can eat, drink, or bathe in them to take advantage of their cleansing properties.

What You Need

Baking sheet

Ingredients

1 cup beech mushrooms

3 lemons

1 cup white vinegar

4 sprigs fresh thyme

$^1/_2$ cup sea salt

Spell Instructions

1. Before you begin your spell, dry your beech mushrooms.

2. Begin by laying your mushrooms on a baking sheet in a single layer.

3. Dry the mushrooms at 150 degrees for approximately an hour.

4. Flip the mushrooms over, and continue to dry for another hour.

5. Remove, and let cool.

6. While the mushrooms are cooling, cut your lemons into rounds and begin to run your bath.

7. Once your bath is full and the mushrooms are cooled, step in front of the bath with all of your ingredients, and begin to ground by envisioning a white light glowing from the top of your head, then dripping down your entire body inch by inch.

8. Sprinkle a handful of mushrooms, lemons, vinegar, thyme, and sea salt into the bath.

9. Soak in the tub while envisioning your aura becoming purified with white light.

10. When you feel you are ready, remove the plug from the tub and stay inside, watching all the negative energy flow down the drain.

11. Step out of the bath and send your white light into the universe.

12. While it may seem counterintuitive, do not rinse your body, but be sure to remove all remnants of your ingredients. Collect what is left in the tub and discard it.

13. Make sure you sleep right after this spell if you don't want to smell like vinegar in a social situation! You may resume showering the next day.

Other Variations

If you do not own a bathtub, you can make a smaller batch of this mixture and anoint yourself with it while in the shower, following the same rules. Portobello may be used as a substitute for beech mushrooms.

GLAMOUR

Glamour magick is the use of beauty to strengthen your confidence and conjure up a specific intention. One may recall the spell in *The Craft* when Robin Tunney changes her hair color; while swiping your hands over your locks may not produce the same effects, dying it red may give you a sultrier energy, and that could be considered glamour magick. In the same way, swiping on hot-pink lipstick may help you feel flirtatious and adventurous. Wearing blue jewelry may help you better communicate your feelings. Using intention in mundane routine, such as applying cosmetics, jewelry, or getting dressed in the morning, can have incredible results.

How Can Mushrooms Help?

Mushrooms, while a delightful and often edible ingredient, are not just for kitchen witchery. They can also be used as a fabric dye. Certain species of mushrooms have incredibly bright, vibrant colors that can be used when practicing color magick, which is the correspondence of colors to the energy they invoke. For example, yellow is associated with joy and creativity, so if you were to wear yellow makeup before a school project, it could help get your creative juices flowing. Cloth dyed in vibrant colors can have the same effect, so by dying a scarf yellow in the spell below, one can enjoy not only the energetic benefits of the color but also the correspondences of the mushroom used to create the dye.

What You Need

Small bowl

Large stainless steel pot

"Prepared for dye" silk scarf

Ingredients

Aluminum acetate mordant (use ten percent of silk scarf weight)

12 ounces hen of the woods mushroom (or 3:1 to fabric weight)

Spell Instructions

1. Make sure you are preparing this dye in a well-ventilated area.

2. To prepare for your spell, parse out the necessary amount of mordant, and add it to a small bowl of warm water. Stir well until it is dissolved.

3. Fill your pot with enough water to soak your scarf, and add in the mordant, but don't add the other ingredients yet. The amount of water doesn't have to be exact—just make sure there is enough room in the pot so that you do not spill.

4. Put the pot on the stove, and bring the water to between 140 and 160 degrees.

5. Once your water reaches the desired temperature, add the mushrooms.

6. Stepping away from the pot with all of your materials near you, begin to ground by envisioning a white light emanating from the top of your head down to your toes.

7. Take your scarf and rinse it for about twenty minutes in warm water, all the while imbuing it with the intention of happiness.

8. Wring out the scarf, and place it in the pot.

9. Let your mixture simmer for about an hour, occasionally stirring in the intention of joy and creativity in a clockwise motion.

10. Remove from heat, and check the pigment of your scarf. If it is too muted, let it soak overnight in the dye mixture.

11. Once the desired color is achieved, let the scarf dry naturally. Once dry, adorn yourself with this scarf while imagining the intention of cheer.

Other Variations

Since this spell works with the hen of the woods mushroom, it creates a yellow pigment, which is aligned with joy and creativity. However, different mushrooms will allow for different colors, and other mordants will either enrich or mute said color. For example, oyster mushrooms exude a gray-green pigment, which can be good for modest abundance. Reishi creates a rust red, which is aligned with a grounded passion. One may also use this dye for wool skeins, and even cotton, but it is easiest for beginners to use a fabric that is already prepared for dye.

PSYCHIC PROTECTION

Psychic protection is the art of maintaining a grounded mental state. In fact, this should be one of the first practices a budding witch should embark on. We are all susceptible to being knocked off our cerebral game, whether we are blindsided by a confrontation or, more metaphysically, when experiencing a nightmare that results in sleep paralysis. The latter is believed by some to be a result of astral travel by an inexperienced witch, or the work of a spirit trying to come into contact with a sleeping host. Whatever your basis of belief is, however, it is wise to strengthen your grounding abilities whether performing spellwork or simply existing.

How Can Mushrooms Help?

Because of their innate grounding properties, derived from their earth-bound existence, mushrooms are great psychic anchors. To amplify this power even more, use a variety of mushroom that corre-sponds with protection. And while enjoy-ing a mushroom dish is an excellent way to invoke psychic protection, you can also dry your fungus and create a small magickal satchel to carry, place on an altar, or keep under your pillow to aid in defense. While meditation and

mental health are the strongest practices a witch can employ to aid in psychic protection, an intentional collection of herbs and items can really intensify the effects of whatever else you are doing to guard your energy.

What You Need

Baking sheet

Mortar and pestle

Nonporous pouch

Ingredients

1 handful of black trumpet mushrooms

Black salt (or prepare your own with a mortar and pestle using sea salt and black pepper)

Pepper

Small piece of obsidian

Dash of anise

Dash of cloves

Dash of dried basil

Spell Instructions

1. Before you begin your spell, dry your black trumpet mushrooms to extend their shelf life. Like all of the other dried mushroom blends in this book, this one is also a tasty item to keep around, so while you'll only need a handful, feel free to make a big batch to keep some on hand.

2. Begin by laying your mushrooms on a baking sheet in a single layer.

3. Dry the mushrooms at 150 degrees for approximately an hour.

4. Flip the mushrooms over, and continue to cook for another hour.

5. Remove from the oven and let cool.

6. If preparing your own black salt, do so now by mixing your sea salt and pepper with a mortar and pestle until it is fully combined.

7. Once everything is prepared and cooled, take all of your ingredients, including the obsidian, into your space and ground into yourself by envisioning a white light emanating from your third eye, illuminating all of your objects. Sit with this light for as long as feels comfortable.

8. Fill your pouch with all your ingredients.

9. Sit with your pouch in your hands and keep the white light glowing from your third eye. Ask for protection from your guides.

10. When you feel ready, knot your bag three times, and send your white light into the universe.

11. Keep this bag on your person, your altar, or under your pillow for extra protection on the astral plane.

Other Variations

All mushrooms have an earthbound property, which makes them great for grounding. While black trumpet has the added benefit of an absorbing nature, any mushroom will help anchor the practitioner. Because psychic attacks occur in the mind, bridging the gap between earth and metaphysical is the correct approach to protection.

WARD

Similar to psychic protection, a ward is a magickal defense. However, it is generally directed at present harm, used as a sort of force field in order to block out any negativity sent your way. For example, if having a negative run-in with an acquaintance has sparked a string of bad luck, you may be in need of a ward. Even if the person is not a practicing witch, sometimes repetitive ill-wishing can be enough direction for the universe. However, wards can also be preventative, and they are often more successful when used in this way as opposed to being used to reverse negative energy.

How Can Mushrooms Help?

By definition, a mushroom is a fungus, which is an organism that often exists parasitically or symbiotically with another organism. When working with a ward, choosing a parasitic mushroom will help the spell feast on the negativity that has entered your sphere. If used in a preventative way, it will do the same with anything crossing your path.

Because of this property, it is also an excellent ingredient for a hex, but because these two spells are different in a nuanced way, it is very important to make sure your intention as a practitioner is clear when you cast either one.

What You Need

Baking sheet

Mortar and pestle

Doormat

Ingredients

1 ounce black trumpet mushrooms

1 ounce sea salt

1 ounce dried rosemary

Spell Instructions

1. Before you begin your spell, dry your black trumpet mushrooms.

2. Begin by laying the mushrooms on a baking sheet in a single layer.

3. Dry the mushrooms at 150 degrees for approximately one hour.

4. Flip the mushrooms over, and continue to cook for another hour.

5. Remove and let cool.

6. When your mushrooms are dried and cool, add sea salt and rosemary into your mortar, and crush with your pestle until mixed to your liking.

7. Sprinkle this mixture under your doormat while asking your guides for protection, and keep it there for as long as you desire.

Other Variations

If there are children or animals in your home, it may be wise to keep these ingredients out of their reach. To do so, place your ingredients in a satchel or jar and hang it over your front door. If you live in a house, you may want to sprinkle this mixture around the perimeter of your land, starting at the northernmost corner and moving clockwise. If you share a home and/or live in an apartment, you can perform this action around your room. While black trumpet mushrooms are ideal, use of any other easily procured mushroom will add a grounding property to your ward.

HEALING

A healing spell is often misconstrued as a be-all and end-all for medical care; this couldn't be further from the truth. A healing spell is an aid, albeit a powerful one, but it cannot substitute for traditional medical care. But, whether you were privy to it or not, you may have been given a healing spell by your caregiver when you were young and had a cold, possibly in the form of a lemon tea—a potent beverage because of both its ingredients and the intention that motivated your caregiver to serve it to you. While modern medicine may have been prescribed, the tea played an important role in terms of fortifying your immune system, as well as being soothing to your discomfort. Herbalism is a large piece of healing magick and has been since ancient times. Now we can couple it with contemporary medicine and marvel at the results as they unfold.

How Can Mushrooms Help?

Mushrooms have a variety of medicinal properties, including, purportedly, antifungal, anticancer, antibiotic, and anti-inflammatory aspects (among others) that aid in holistic healing. Ancient medicine from China, Russia, and more has parlayed its way into modern times through the increased popularity of using dehydrated mushrooms to aid in the healing process. When you are feeling under the weather, a smoothie with lots of healing agents, including mushrooms, is a great way to aid your immune system in its fight against bacterial attackers.

What You Need

Blender or food processor

Ingredients

1 cup vanilla almond milk

1 tablespoon coconut oil

A handful enoki mushrooms

2 cups fresh spinach

1 banana

1 cup berries

1 pinch black pepper

Spell Instructions

1. Make sure all of your ingredients are washed and prepared carefully before beginning your spell.

2. Start by grounding with your ingredients before you. You can ground by envisioning roots growing from where your feet touch the floor into the center of the earth. This will anchor you.

3. Begin by adding your almond milk into your food processor or blender, asking for healing.

4. Add your coconut oil, envisioning yourself as the picture of health.

5. Continue to add each ingredient one by one, asking for the essence of healing.

6. Begin to blend your ingredients together, envisioning yourself in your healthiest form, letting the ingredients swim together.

7. Pour into a glass, enjoy, and, while drinking, follow the sensation of your smoothie down your throat and through your body, feeling it give you energy and health.

Other Variations

This is an extremely flexible spell that can be adjusted, depending upon your taste buds. Enoki mushrooms are very mild in flavor, so they shouldn't be too overpowering, but there are other mushrooms, such as chaga and reishi, that can also work well without adding a strong flavor. You might also want to use a mushroom with a more specific intention beyond achieving or maintaining good health. For example, if your healing intention is geared toward being healthy for work, you could substitute a mushroom that is more aligned with abundance, such as cremini, porcini, or hen of the woods.

VITALITY

A vitality spell can mean one of two things: it can energize you in general, or it can kick-start your libido. In ancient times, vitality spells were associated with immortality, but no witch in history (to my knowledge) has achieved endless life, so it is safe to assume that the metaphor is just that. However, when calling in more energy for your daily activities, or even upping the ante in the bedroom, these spells can be incredibly powerful. Whether the practitioner is looking to spark the creative juices or spice up romantic endeavors, vitality spells can be excellent to provide the extra oomph.

How Can Mushrooms Help?

The first two sections of this book extensively covered how important mushrooms were to ancient civilizations in their search for immortality. Rituals were held across the globe in unique ways that centered around use of mushrooms for prolonging life or adding the appearance or energy of youth. These kinds of centuries-old rites have imbued the mushroom with powerful meaning, and the echo of that meaning lives in these organisms to the present day, making them the perfect ingredients to add verve to your daily activities. And of course, beyond even spiritual significance, mushrooms are full of healthy nutrients that have made them vital as sustenance throughout time.

What You Need

Baking sheet

Food processor

Shaker and strainer

Rocks glass

Ingredients

$1/2$ pound fresh shiitake mushrooms, or $1\ 1/2$ ounces dried, for powder

1 tablespoon red pepper flakes

$2/3$ cup Himalayan salt

2 tablespoons dried oregano

1 teaspoon black pepper

1 ounce fresh lime juice

$1/4$ ounce agave

$1\ 1/2$ ounces mezcal

$1/4$ ounce fresh squeezed orange juice

Ice

Cut limes

Tajin for rim

Spell Instructions

1. Before you begin your spell, dry your mushrooms.

2. Begin by laying your mushrooms on a baking sheet in a single layer.

3. Dry the mushrooms at 150 degrees for approximately one hour.

4. Flip the mushrooms over, and continue to cook for another hour.

5. Remove and let cool.

6. Once cooled, take 1 ½ ounces or 3 tablespoons of the dried shiitake mushrooms, red pepper flakes, salt, oregano, and black pepper, and add into a food processor, pulsing until it creates a fine powder.

7. Now that you have your powder, place all of your tools in front of you and begin to ground by envisioning a white light that glows from the top of your head, dripping down your entire body inch by inch.

8. Fill your shaker with ice, and add the lime juice, agave, mezcal, orange juice, and ½ teaspoon of your mushroom powder.

9. Begin to shake vigorously while envisioning a deep red light emanating from your sacral chakra, sitting just below your belly button. Keep shaking until you feel the energy flowing through you.

10. Take a lime and rim your rocks glass with it clockwise while envisioning what vitality means to you. Place the tajin on a small plate, and dip the glass into it, creating a spiced rim.

11. Fill your rocks glass with ice, and strain your cocktail.

12. As you imbibe, envision your intention of vitality and enjoy responsibly.

Other Variations

Shiitake is regarded in Asian culture as the mushroom of immortality across history. It also has a robust enough taste to compete in this cocktail, standing up to the assertive flavor of mezcal, which was used by the Aztecs to achieve enlightenment alongside sacred mushrooms. Purchased mushroom powders can work well in lieu of the one described above. Finally, if you would prefer indulging sans alcohol, you may perform the spell without mezcal, substituting soda water to make a great nonalcoholic version.

Bibliography

"Aboriginal Use of Fungi." Fungi, Australian Fungi, copyright 2012. https://www
.anbg.gov.au/fungi/aboriginal.html.

Blaszczak-Boxe, Agata. "Prehistoric High Times: Early Humans Used Magic
Mushrooms, Opium." News, Live Science, February 2. 2015. https://www
.livescience.com/49666-prehistoric-humans-psychoactive-drugs.html.

"Chanterelle Mushrooms." Mushrooms, Speciality Produce, copyright
1996–2021. https://specialtyproduce.com/produce/Chanterelle_Mushrooms
_705.php.

"Dyeing with Mushrooms." *Bloom & Dye*, January 31, 2019. https://www
.bloomanddye.com/journal/2019/2/1/dyeing-with-mushrooms.

"Dyeing with Mushrooms," Mushroom-Collecting.com, copyright 2011. http://
mushroom-collecting.com/mushroomdyeing.html.

Editors of Encyclopedia Britannica. "Soma." Religious Beliefs, Britannica. https://
www.britannica.com/topic/soma-Hinduism.

El Enshasy, Hesham, Ramlan Aziz, and Mohamad A. Wadaan. "Mushrooms and
Truffles: Historical Biofactories for Complementary Medicine in Africa and in the
Middle East" 2013, *Hindawi*, November 20, 2013. https://www.hindawi.com
/journals/ecam/2013/620451/.

Lu, Emma. "Legend of the Spiritual Lingzhi Mushroom of Immortality." Nspirement, July 3, 2017. https://www.nspirement.com/2017/07/03/legend-of-the-spiritual-lingzhi-mushroom-of-immortality.html.

"Mushrooms as Sacred Objects in North America." *Cornell Mushroom Blog*, January 6, 2010. https://blog.mycology.cornell.edu/2010/01/06/mushrooms-as-sacred-objects-in-north-america/.

"Mushrooms and Truffles: Historical Biofactories for Complementary Medicine in Africa and in the Middle East," Volume 2013, *Hindawi*, November 20, 2013, https://www.hindawi.com/journals/ecam/2013/620451/.

Oso, B. A. *Mushrooms and the Yoruba People of Nigeria*. London: Taylor & Francis 1975.

"Prehistoric High Times: Early Humans Used Magic Mushrooms, Opium," News, Live Science, February 2, 2015, https://www.livescience.com/49666-prehistoric-humans-psychoactive-drugs.html.

"Soma," Religious Beliefs, Brittanica, https://www.britannica.com/topic/soma-Hinduism.

"Teonanacatl Mushrooms: Flesh of the Gods." Plants of Mind and Spirit, U.S. Forest Service. https://www.fs.fed.us/wildflowers/ethnobotany/Mind_and_Spirit/teonanacatl.shtml.

Truttman, Peter. *The Forgotten Mushrooms of Ancient Peru*. Oreslina, Switzerland: Global Mountain Action, 2012.

Wilbert, J., and K. Simoneau, eds. *Folk Literature of the Cuiva Indians*. Los Angeles: UCLA Latin American Center Publications, 1991.

About the Author

Shawn Engel, owner of Witchy Wisdoms, is a spiritual mentor, brand strategist, six-figure CEO, and published author. She has been featured in multiple publications including *Cosmopolitan*, *Bust*, and *The Daily Mail*, and is the author of *Cosmopolitan: Love Spells and Witch's Brew* (both Sterling), and *The Power of Hex* (Chicago Review). She recently founded the Boss Mystic Podcast Network, which is a growing home to witchcraft podcasts, including two of her own, *The Boss Mystic* and *True Crime Astrology*.

Find her online at witchywisdoms.com.